Quel

We thank God for
your presence in
Our lives. You have
loved and taught
us so much!

The Swopes

REFLECTIVE LIVING SERIES

# Reflections *on the* Word

## DEVOTIONAL

*Meditating on God's Word in the
Everyday Moments of Life*

# KEN GIRE

**Chariot Victor Publishing**
A Division of Cook Communications

Chariot Victor Publishing
A division of Cook Communications, Colorado Springs, Colorado 80918
Cook Communications, Paris, Ontario
Kingsway Communications, Eastbourne, England

REFLECTIONS ON THE WORD
© 1998 by Ken Gire. All rights reserved
Printed in the United States of America

Editor: Greg Clouse
Cover and Interior Design: D² DesignWorks

1 2 3 4 5 6 7 8 9 10 Printing / Year 02 01 00 99 98

CIP data applied for

Before this time my practice had been, at least for ten years previously, as an habitual thing, to give myself to prayer after having dressed in the morning. Now, I saw that the most important thing was to give myself to reading God's Word, *and to meditation on it,* that thus my heart might be comforted, encouraged, warned, reproved, instructed. . . .

*The first thing I did,* after having asked in a few words of the Lord's blessing upon his precious Word, *was to begin to meditate on the Word of God,* searching as it were into every verse to get blessing out of it; not for the sake of the public ministry of the Word, not for the sake of preaching on what I had meditated upon, but for the sake of obtaining food for my own soul.

The result I have found to be almost invariably this, that after a few minutes my soul has been led to confession, or to thanksgiving, or to intercession, or to supplication; so that, though I did not, as it were, give myself to prayer, *but to meditation,* yet it turned almost immediately more or less to prayer. When thus I have been for a while making confession or intercession or supplication, or have given thanks, I go on to the next words or verse, turning all, as I go on, into prayer for myself or others, as the Word may lead to it, but still continually keeping before me that food for my own soul is the object of my meditation. The result of this is that . . . my inner man almost invariably is even sensibly nourished and strengthened. . . .

George Mueller
*spring 1841, Bristol, England*

*How blessed is the man who does not walk in the counsel of the wicked, nor stand in the path of sinners, nor sit in the seat of scoffers! But his delight is in the law of the Lord, and in His law he meditates day and night. And he will be like a tree firmly planted by streams of water, which yields its fruit in its season, and its leaf does not wither; and in whatever he does, he prospers.*

PSALM 1:1-3

# INTRODUCTION

The Bible begins and ends in Paradise. In between the garden of Eden and the garden in the New Jerusalem lies a sprawling landscape.

In the life of Israel, the landscape stretches from Ur to Egypt, winds around Mount Sinai, through a wilderness, into a land flowing with milk and honey, out into exile, and eventually back to Palestine.

The life of Christ traces other terrain. There is a wilderness, too, only a different one. And heavenly words are also revealed on a mountain, only not on tablets of stone but in words of a sermon, words that give those spoken on Mount Sinai even greater resonance. On another mountain, a higher mountain, His glory is revealed. There is a valley through which He passes, a garden in which He prays, and a hill on which He dies.

The life of the church has its own unique landscape. The peaks of Pentecost. The valleys of Corinth. The plateaus of Laodicea.

Our own lives, yours and mine, pass through a similar geography of the soul, with its pinnacles of faith and its valleys of doubt, its plateaus of complacency, its wildernesses of spiritual dryness.

Along the way, God speaks. In the peak experiences of our lives. In the valleys. On the plateaus. Even in the wilderness, where all traces of Him seem to have vanished. And who knows but that what we hear along the way may be just the word we need at that particular juncture of our spiritual journey. To walk us through some fearful valley to a place of pasture. To lead us out of some wilderness so we can lie down by still waters.

To help find out how God may be speaking to you, I have tried to encourage you in the art of meditating on His Word. For if you learn to hear Him there, you will likely learn to hear Him elsewhere.

He has much to say, not only from the Scriptures but from the circumstances of our everyday lives. However prosaic the pages of our lives may seem at first reading, within the lines or in between the lines God may be speaking. Every book we read, every movie we see, every person we talk with, every song we listen to, every moment in our lives, in fact, should be subjects for reflection and could be ways through which God is speaking.

If we travel too fast, though, we'll likely miss it. So if we want to hear what the Word of God is saying to us, first we have to slow down. That is what the format of *Reflections on the Word* is designed to do. To create pauses for reflection. The pauses are something like park benches so you can stop and sit and reflect on your own spiritual journey. To check the map. And your bearings. And to make any adjustments in your course.

We'll start each daily devotional with "*Reading* the Word." That will be followed by a section called "*Reflecting* on the

Word" which offers insight into the biblical passage. Written by people from around the world and across the centuries, these insights come from such spiritual guides as Richard Foster or Mother Teresa, A.W. Tozer or C.S. Lewis, Frederick Buechner or Philip Yancey, Edith Schaeffer or Eugene Peterson. The goal here is not academic analysis but spiritual illumination, to raise the lamp of the Word a little higher so it will shine a little brighter on whatever path you are presently traveling.

The section labeled "*Responding* to the Word" takes the reading and the reflection and makes them personal, allowing your time in the Word to find its way into your life. The prayer is designed only to start you praying, in hopes that the Holy Spirit will bring other things to mind, other vistas He would have you see, other paths He would have you take, other precipices He would have you avoid.

By allowing these spiritual guides to accompany you on your own journey, you will be mentored along the way in the art of biblical meditation. Sit with them on that park bench for a few minutes, and when you do, still your heart to listen. For sometimes the voice of God thunders into our lives, but, more often than not, it wisps by us like a gentle breeze with a fragrant reminder in it of faraway fields.

So take your time, relax, and reflect . . .

not only on the biblical landscape

but on the landscape of your life.

# Reflections *on the* Word

DEVOTIONAL

❧

In my book, *The Reflective Life*, the primer in the series, I introduce three habits of the heart that nurture a reflective life: *reading* the moment, *reflecting* on the moment, and *responding* to the moment. In this devotional, they are specifically applied to what we see in the Scriptures:

> *Reading the Word* is using our eyes to see what's on the surface.

> *Reflecting on the Word* is engaging our mind to see what's beneath the surface.

> *Responding to the Word* is giving what we have seen a place to live in our heart, allowing it to grow there, upward to God and outward to other people.

Ken Gire

### *Reading* the Word

In the beginning God created the heavens and the earth. And the earth was formless and void, and darkness was over the surface of the deep; and the Spirit of God was moving over the surface of the waters. Then God said, "Let there be light"; and there was light. *(Genesis 1:1-3)*

### *Reflecting* on the Word

Eons ago, the Spirit of God hovered over the nest of the new earth, working with the Word of God to bring form and fullness to the creation. The mechanics of the miracle remain a mystery. "Just as you do not know the path of the wind and how bones are formed in the womb of a pregnant woman," said Solomon, "so you do not know the activity of God who makes all things."

Going from the miracle of physical life to the miracle of spiritual life, the mystery remains. "The wind blows where it wishes and you hear the sound of it, but do not know where it comes from or where it is going," Jesus said. "So is everyone born of the Spirit."

The Spirit of God that moved over the waters of the young earth, that moved over the womb of a young virgin, still moves today. Just as miraculously. And just as mysteriously.

Our response, it seems to me, should be awe, not analysis; worship, not reasoning; joy, not jury duty on the way God has chosen to work in the world He has created.

Ken Gire

## *Responding* to the Word

Creator Spirit, who broodest everlastingly over the lands and waters of the earth, enduing them with forms and colours which no human skill can copy, give me to-day, I beseech Thee, the mind and heart to rejoice in Thy creation.

Forbid that I should walk through Thy beautiful world with unseeing eyes:

Forbid that the lure of the market-place should ever entirely steal my heart away from the love of the open acres and the green trees:

Forbid that under the low roof of workshop or office or study I should ever forget Thy great overarching sky:

Forbid that when all Thy creatures are greeting the morning with songs and shouts of joy, I alone should wear a dull and sullen face:

Let the energy and vigour which in Thy wisdom Thou hast infused into every living thing stir to-day within my being, that I may not be among Thy creatures as a sluggard and a drone:

And above all give me grace to use these beauties of earth without me and this eager stirring of life within me as a means whereby my soul may rise from creature to Creator, and from nature to nature's God.

John Baillie
*A Diary of Private Prayer*

### *Reading* the Word

Then God said, "Let the earth bring forth living creatures after their kind: cattle and creeping things and beasts of the earth after their kind"; and it was so. And God made the beasts of the earth after their kind, and the cattle after their kind, and everything that creeps on the ground after its kind; and God saw that it was good. Then God said, "Let Us make man in Our image, according to Our likeness; and let them rule over the fish of the sea and over the birds of the sky and over the cattle and over all the earth, and over every creeping thing that creeps on the earth." *(Genesis 1:24-26)*

12

### *Reflecting* on the Word

In the Old Testament animals are often thought of with affection. Thus, the commandment about the Sabbath mandated that animals, too, should have rest on feast days. It is expressly forbidden that the ox who stamps out the grain on the threshing floor should have his mouth bound. Later, the Apostle Paul, in a marvelous passage in his letter to the Romans, describes how even the creatures sigh with us to be freed from anxiety and perishability.

Albert Schweitzer
*A Place for Revelation*

## *Responding* to the Word

O God, I thank thee
for all the creatures thou hast made,
so perfect in their kind—
great animals like the elephant and the rhinoceros,
humorous animals like the camel and the monkey,
friendly ones like the dog and the cat,
working ones like the horse and the ox,
timid ones like the squirrel and the rabbit,
majestic ones like the lion and the tiger,
for birds with their songs.
O Lord give us such love for thy creation,
that love may cast out fear,
and all thy creatures see in man
their priest and friend,
through Jesus Christ our Lord.

George Appleton
*The Oxford Book of Prayer*

## *Reading* the Word

God created man in His own image, in the image of God He created him; male and female He created them. *(Genesis 1:27)*

We are His workmanship, created in Christ Jesus for good works. . . . *(Ephesians 2:10)*

## *Reflecting* on the Word

We are, not metaphorically but in very truth, a Divine work of art, something that God is making, and therefore something with which He will not be satisfied until it has a certain character. Here again we come against what I have called the "intolerable compliment." Over a sketch made idly to amuse a child, an artist may not take much trouble: he may be content to let it go even though it is not exactly as he meant it to be. But over the great picture of his life—the work which he loves, though in a different fashion, as intensely as a man loves a woman or a mother a child—he will take endless trouble—and would, doubtless, thereby give endless trouble to the picture if it were sentient. One can imagine a sentient picture, after being rubbed and scraped and re-commenced for the tenth time, wishing that it were only a thumb-nail sketch whose making was over in a minute. In the same way, it is natural for us to wish that God had designed us for a less glorious and less arduous destiny, but then we are wishing not for more love but for less.

C.S. Lewis

*The Problem of Pain*

14

## *Responding* to the Word

Eternal Father, you said, "Let us make humankind to our own image and likeness." Thus you were willing to share with us your own greatness. You gave us the intellect to share your truth. You gave us the wisdom to share your goodness. And you gave us the free will to love that which is true and just.

Why did you so dignify us? It was because you looked upon us, and fell in love with us. It was love which first prompted you to create us; and it was love which caused you to share with us your truth and goodness.

Yet your heart must break when you see us turn against you. You must weep when you see us abusing our intellect in pursuit of that which is false. You must cry with pain when we distort our wisdom in order to justify evil.

But you never desert us. Out of the same love that caused you to create us, you have now sent your only Son to save us. He is your perfect image and likeness, and so through his we can be restored to your image and likeness.

15

Catherine of Siena
*Book of Prayers*
compiled by Robert Van de Weyer

### *Reading* the Word

And they heard the sound of the Lord God walking in the garden in the cool of the day, and the man and his wife hid themselves from the presence of the Lord God among the trees of the garden. Then the Lord God called to the man, and said to him, "Where are you?" *(Genesis 3:8-9)*

### *Reflecting* on the Word

Those who recall Francis Thompson's haunting image of God as the Hound of Heaven, pursuing us down the halls of time, might well ask who, in fact, is the hound and who the quarry, whether we seek God or whether we are sought. If we try to answer the question on those terms, however, we stray into theological foolishness. What we discover, instead, is that all the while we have been pursuing God, he has been rushing toward us with reckless love, arms flung wide to hug us home. God aches for every person, for every creature, indeed, for every scrap of life in all creation to be joined again in the unity that was its first destiny. So while we are crying out, "Where are you, God?" the divine voice echoes through our hiding places, "Where are you?" Indeed, the story of the Garden of Eden reminds us that it is God who calls out first, and to this we answer. God's yearning for us stirs up our longing in response. God's initiating presence may be ever so subtle—an inward tug of desire, a more-than-coincidence meeting of words and events, a glimpse of the

16

beyond in a storm or in a flower—but it is enough to make the heart skip a beat and to make us want to know more.

Howard Macy

*Rhythms of the Inner Life*

### *Responding* to the Word

For your heart that loves me,
For your feet that pursue me,
For your voice that calls out to me,
I thank you, O God.
Thank you for raising the questions
that draw me into a dialogue with you
about my life and how I have been living it.
Thank you for every tug of conscience
that has led to every timid step
that has brought me out in the open
in my relationship with you.
My hope, O God, my only hope,
is that you are more persistent in your seeking
than I am in my hiding.

Ken Gire

## *Reading* the Word

Now the Lord said to Abram,
"Go forth from your country,
And from your relatives
And from your father's house,
To the land which I will show you;
And I will make you a great nation,
And I will bless you,
And make your name great;
And so you shall be a blessing;
And I will bless those who bless you,
And the one who curses you I will curse.
And in you all the families of the earth shall be blessed."

So Abram went forth as the Lord had spoken to him; and Lot went with him. Now Abram was seventy-five years old when he departed from Haran. *(Genesis 12:1-4)*

## *Reflecting* on the Word

In packing up his belongings and moving his family across the desert, Abram was taking the first step in what was to become the all-time classic life of faith. He was in addition to set in motion a stream of history which would change the Western world for three millennia, would allow Abram to contribute through his descendants more to modern music, drama, science and banking than any other man and would remain at the center stage of world history at the end of time. From his loins would spring not only kings and prophets but the redeemer of the world. It is impossible to estimate the effects on human history of Abram's decision to leave Haran.

But Abram had no means of foreseeing, let alone understanding Einsteinian physics, Rothsteinian banking or two thousand years of church history. He had but the word of God and the promise of a destiny. His decision to move out, sacrifice or no sacrifice, was essentially a gamble of faith. He trusted God that there were better things for him than lay in Haran.

I do not know what your Haran is. To leave it may be a less traumatic decision than Abram's. But in its way it will be just as momentous.

John White
*The Cost of Commitment*

### *Responding* to the Word

Dear God,

Someone once said that writing a novel is like driving at night with your headlights on—you can only see a few feet ahead, but you can make the entire trip that way. Living a life is like that, too, I think. Certainly a life of faith. Give me the grace, O God, to live such a life . . . and to realize that though the light given me is never as much as I would like, it is enough. It is enough.

Ken Gire

### *Reading* the Word

Then Jacob was left alone, and a man wrestled with him until daybreak. . . . And he said, "Your name shall no longer be Jacob, but Israel; for you have striven with God and with me and have prevailed." *(Genesis 32:24, 28)*

### *Reflecting* on the Word

"Heel grabber" is what Jacob's name means, a name you would expect of a wrestler. Jacob's entire life up till now was spent calculating his next move and maneuvering to a position of advantage so he could pry from God's hands so many of the blessings that God in time had wanted to give him anyway.

Now it was God's turn to grab Jacob's heel, to wrestle with this fundamental flaw in his nature, and touch him in a way so he would never forget the encounter. Through the ordeal, Jacob learned that God's blessing comes not from grabbing but from clinging.

There is something of Jacob in all of us, I think. If so, there must be a night of reckoning for us as well. A night when God finds us alone, grabs us, throws us to the ground, and wrestles with that fundamental flaw in our character. In that dark night of the soul, though He cripples us, in the dawn He blesses us.

For some of us, the crippling *is* the blessing.

Ken Gire

### *Responding* to the Word

O persistent God,
deliver me from assuming your mercy is gentle.
Pressure me that I may grow more human,
not through the lessening of my struggles,
but through an expansion of them. . . .
Deepen my hurt
until I learn to share it and myself openly,
and my needs honestly.
Sharpen my fears until I name them
and release the power I have locked in them
and they in me.
Accentuate my confusion
until I shed those grandiose expectations
that divert me from the small, glad gifts
of the now and the here and the me.
Expose my shame where it shivers,
crouched behind the curtains of propriety,
until I can laugh at last
through my common frailties and failures,
laugh my way toward becoming whole.

21

Ted Loder
*Guerrillas of Grace*

## *Reading* the Word

Meanwhile little Samuel was helping the Lord by assisting Eli. Messages from the Lord were very rare in those days, but one night after Eli had gone to bed (he was almost blind with age by now), and Samuel was sleeping in the Temple near the Ark, the Lord called out, "Samuel! Samuel!"

"Yes?" Samuel replied. "What is it?" He jumped up and ran to Eli. "Here I am. What do you want?" he asked.

"I didn't call you," Eli said. "Go on back to bed." So he did. Then the Lord called again, "Samuel!" And again Samuel jumped up and ran to Eli.

"Yes?" he asked. "What do you need?"

"No, I didn't call you, my son," Eli said. "Go on back to bed."

(Samuel had never had a message from Jehovah before.) So now the Lord called the third time, and once more Samuel jumped up and ran to Eli.

"Yes?" he asked. "What do you need?"

Then Eli realized it was the Lord who had spoken to the child. So he said to Samuel, "Go and lie down again, and if he calls again, say, 'Yes, Lord, I'm listening.'" So Samuel went back to bed.

And the Lord came and called as before, "Samuel! Samuel!"

And Samuel replied, "Yes, I'm listening." *(1 Samuel 3:1-10, TLB)*

### *Reflecting* on the Word

If we knew how to listen to God, we would hear him speaking to us. For God does speak. He speaks in his Gospels. He also speaks through life—that new gospel to which we ourselves add a page each day. . . . If we knew how to listen to God, if we knew how to look around us, our whole life would become prayer.

Michel Quoist
*Prayers*

### *Responding* to the Word

Speak, Lord, for your servant is listening. . . .

In days gone by the children of Israel said to Moses, "Speak to us and we shall listen; do not let the Lord speak to us, lest we die." This is not how I pray, Lord. No. With the great prophet Samuel, I humbly and earnestly beg: "Speak, Lord, for your servant is listening."

So, do not let Moses speak to me, but you, O Lord, my God, eternal Truth, you speak to me. If I hear your voice, may I not be condemned for hearing the word and not following it, for knowing it and not loving it, or believing it and not living it. Speak then, Lord, for your servant listens, for you have the words of eternal life. Speak to me to comfort my soul and to change my whole life; in turn, may it give you praise and glory and honor, forever and ever. Amen.

Thomas à Kempis

### *Reading* the Word

The Lord is my rock and my fortress and my deliverer;
My God, my rock, in whom I take refuge;
My shield and the horn of my salvation. . . . *(2 Samuel 22:2-3)*

### *Reflecting* on the Word

I arise today with the power of God to guide me,
The might of God to uphold me,
The wisdom of God to teach me,
The eye of God to watch over me,
The ear of God to hear me,
The word of God to give me speech,
The hand of God to protect me,
The way of God to prevent me,
The shield of God to shelter me,
And the host of God to defend me:
Against the snares of devils,
Against the temptations of vices,
Against the lusts of nature,
Against every man who meditates injury to me,
Whether far or near, with few or with many.

St. Patrick
*Life's Little Prayer Book*
compiled by Gary Lahoda

24

### *Responding* to the Word

Christ, be with me, Christ before me, Christ behind me,

Christ in me, Christ beneath me, Christ above me,

Christ on my right, Christ on my left,

Christ where I lie, Christ where I sit, Christ where I arise,

Christ in the heart of every one who thinks of me,

Christ in the mouth of every one who speaks of me,

Christ in every eye that sees me

Christ in every ear that hears me.

Salvation is of the Lord.

Salvation is of the Lord.

Salvation is of the Christ.

May your salvation, O Lord, be ever with us.

St. Patrick's Breastplate

25

## *Reading* the Word

"Why did I not die at birth,
Come forth from the womb and expire?"

"Is not man forced to labor on earth,
And are not his days like the days of a hired man?"

"Why dost Thou hide Thy face,
And consider me Thine enemy?"

"Where now is my hope?" *(Job 3:11; 7:1; 13:24; 17:15a)*

## *Reflecting* on the Word

Be patient toward all that is unsolved in your heart and try to love the questions themselves like locked rooms and like books that are written in a very foreign tongue. Do not now seek the answers, which cannot be given you because you would not be able to live them. And the point is, to live everything. Live the questions now. Perhaps you will then gradually, without noticing it, live along some distant day into the answer.

Rainer Maria Rilke
*Letters to a Young Poet*

## *Responding* to the Word

How shall I pray?
Are tears prayers, Lord?
Are screams prayers,
or groans
or sighs
or curses?
Can trembling hands be lifted to you,
or clenched fists
or the cold sweat that trickles down my back
or the cramps that knot my stomach?
Will you accept my prayers, Lord,
my real prayers,
rooted in the muck and mud and rock of my life,
and not just my pretty, cut-flower, gracefully arranged
bouquet of words?
Will you accept me, Lord,
as I really am,
messed up mixture of glory and grime?

Ted Loder
*Guerrillas of Grace*

27

### *Reading* the Word

For there is hope for a tree,
When it is cut down, that it will sprout again,
And its shoots will not fail.
Though its roots grow old in the ground,
And its stump dies in the dry soil,
At the scent of water it will flourish
And put forth sprigs like a plant. *(Job 14:7-9)*

### *Reflecting* on the Word

28

The tree sends its roots beneath the surface, seeking nourishment in the dark soil: the rich "broken down" matter of life.

As they reach down and search, the roots hold the tree firmly to the earth.

Thus held and nourished, the tree grows upwards into the light, drinking the sun and air and expressing its truth: its branches and foliage, its flowers and fruit. Life swarms around and into it. Birds and insects teem within its embrace, carrying pollen and seed. They nest and breed and sing and buzz. They glorify the creation.

The tree changes as it grows. It is torn by wind and lightning, scarred by frost and fire. Branches die and new ones emerge. The drama of existence has its way with the tree but still it grows; still its roots reach down into the darkness; still its branches flow with sap and reach upward and outward into the world.

A person kneels to contemplate a tree and to reflect upon the troubles and joys of life. The person imagines mornings and evenings in a great forest of prayers, swarming and teeming with life.

The person is learning how to pray.

Michael Leunig
*The Prayer Tree*

### *Responding* to the Word

God help us
To rise up from our struggle.
Like a tree rises up from the soil.
Our roots reaching down to our trouble,
Our rich, dark dirt of existence.
Finding nourishment deeply
And holding us firmly.
Always connected.
Growing upwards and into the sun.
Amen.

Michael Leunig
*The Prayer Tree*

### *Reading* the Word

His hand is heavy despite my groaning.
Oh that I knew where I might find Him,
That I might come to His seat!
I would present my case before Him
And fill my mouth with arguments. . . .
Behold, I go forward but He is not there,
And backward, but I cannot perceive Him;
When He acts on the left, I cannot behold Him;
He turns on the right, I cannot see Him. *(Job 23:2b-4, 8-9)*

30

### *Reflecting* on the Word

One bold message in the Book of Job is that you can say anything
to God. Throw at him your grief, your anger, your doubt, your bitterness, your betrayal, your disappointment—he can absorb them
all. As often as not, spiritual giants of the Bible are shown contend-
ing with God. They prefer to go away limping, like Jacob, rather
than to shut God out. In this respect, the Bible prefigures a tenet of
modern psychology: you can't deny your feelings or make them dis-
appear, so you might as well express them. God can deal with every
human response save one. He cannot abide the response I fall back
on instinctively: an attempt to ignore him or treat him as though
he does not exist. That response never once occurred to Job.

Philip Yancey
*Disappointment with God*

### *Responding* to the Word

God, where are you? . . .
Speak to me! Teach me!
Rebuke me! Strike me down!
But do not remain silent.
The God who is mute. Is that who you are?

You have revealed yourself as the speaking God—
    our communicating Cosmos.
You pointed Abraham to a city whose builder
    and maker was God.
You revealed your divine name to Moses.
You spoke with clarity
to David, to Ruth, to Esther,
to Isaiah, to Ezekiel, to Daniel,
to Mary, to Paul, and a host of others.
Why are the heavens made of iron for me?

Job, I know, experienced you as the hidden God. And Elijah
held a lonely vigil over earthquake, wind, and fire. Me, too.

O God of wonder and mystery, teach me by means of your
wondrous, terrible, loving, all-embracing silence. Amen.

Richard Foster
*Prayers from the Heart*

## *Reading* the Word

My soul is poured out within me;
Days of affliction have seized me.
At night it pierces my bones within me,
And my gnawing pains take no rest. . . .
I cry out to Thee for help, but Thou dost not answer me.
*(Job 30:16-17, 20a)*

## *Reflecting* on the Word

32 I cannot fit it all together by saying, "He did it," but neither can I do so by saying, "There was nothing he could do about it." I cannot fit it all together. I can only, with Job, endure. I do not know why God did not prevent Eric's death. To live without the answer is precarious. It's hard to keep one's footing.

Job's friends tried out on him their answer. "God did it, Job; he was the agent of your children's death. He did it because of some wickedness in you; he did it to punish you. Nothing indeed in your public life would seem to merit such retribution; it must then be something in your private inner life. Tell us what it is, Job. Confess."

The writer of Job refuses to say that God views the lives and deaths of children as cat-o-nine-tails with which to lacerate parents.

I have no explanation. I can do nothing else than endure in the face of this deepest and most painful of mysteries. I believe in God the Father Almighty, maker of heaven and earth and res-urrecter of Jesus Christ. I also believe that my son's life was cut off in its prime. I cannot fit these pieces together. I am at a loss. I have read the theodicies produced to justify the ways of God to man. I find them unconvincing. To the most agonized question I have ever asked I do not know the answer. I do not know why God would watch him fall. I do not know why God would watch me wounded. I cannot even guess.

C.S. Lewis, writing about the death of his wife, was plainly angry with God. He, Lewis, deserved something better than to be treated so shabbily. I am not angry but baffled and hurt. My wound is an unanswered question. The wounds of all humanity are an unanswered question.

33

Nicholas Wolterstorff
*Lament for a Son*

### *Responding* to the Word

He was so young, God. So young and strong and filled with promise. So vital, so radiant, giving so much joy wherever he went. He was so brilliant. On this one boy you lavished so many talents that could have enriched your world. He had already received so many honors, and there were so many honors to come.

Why, then?

In our agony we ask.

Why him?

Marjorie Holmes
*Who Am I, God?*

### *Reading* the Word

In a dream, a vision of the night,
When sound sleep falls on men,
While they slumber in their beds,
Then He opens the ears of men,
And seals their instruction. *(Job 33:15-16)*

### *Reflecting* on the Word

Every once in a while, if you're like me, you have a dream that wakes you up. Sometimes it's a bad dream—a dream in which the shadows become so menacing that your heart skips a beat and you come awake to the knowledge that not even the actual darkness of night is as fearsome as the dreamed darkness, not even the shadows without as formidable as the shadows within. Sometimes it's a sad dream—a dream sad enough to bring real tears to your sleeping eyes so that it's your tears that you wake up by, wake up to. Or again, if you're like me, there are dreams that take a turn so absurd that you wake laughing—as if you need to be awake to savor the full richness of the comedy. Rarest of all is the dream that wakes you with what I can only call its truth.

The path of your dream winds now this way, now that—one scene fades into another, people come and go the way they do in dreams—and then suddenly, deep out of wherever it is that dreams come from, something rises up that shakes you to the foundations. The mystery of the dream suddenly lifts like fog,

34

and for an instant it is as if you glimpse a truth truer than any you knew that you knew if only a truth about yourself. It is too much truth for the dream to hold anyway, and the dream breaks.

Frederick Buechner

*A Room Called Remember*

### *Responding* to the Word

Dear God,

We give thanks for the darkness of the night where lies the world of dreams. Guide us closer to our dreams so that we may be nourished by them. Give us good dreams and memory of them so that we may carry their poetry and mystery into our daily lives.

Grant us deep and restful sleep that we may wake refreshed with strength enough to renew a world grown tired.

We give thanks for the inspiration of stars, the dignity of the moon and the lullabies of crickets and frogs.

Let us restore the night and reclaim it as a sanctuary of peace, where silence shall be music to our hearts and darkness shall throw light upon our souls. Good night. Sweet dreams. Amen.

Michael Leuing

*A Common Prayer*

### *Reading* the Word

Even though I walk through the valley of the shadow of death, I fear no evil; for Thou art with me. *(Psalm 23:4)*

### *Reflecting* on the Word

Most of us do not want valleys in our lives. We shrink from them with a sense of fear and foreboding. Yet in spite of our worst misgivings God can bring great benefit and lasting benediction to others through those valleys. Let us not always try to avoid the dark things, the distressing days. They may well prove to be the way of greatest refreshment to ourselves and those around us. . . .

The shepherd wants to be sure there will not only be water but also the best grazing available for the ewes and their lambs. Generally the choicest meadows are in these valleys along the stream banks. Here the sheep can feed as they move toward the high country.

Naturally these grassy glades are often on the floor of steep-walled canyons and gulches. There may be towering cliffs above them on either side. The valley floor itself may be in dark shadow with the sun seldom reaching the bottom except for a few hours around noon.

The shepherd knows from past experience that predators like coyotes, bears, wolves or cougars can take cover in these broken cliffs and from their vantage point prey on his flock. He knows these valleys can be subject to sudden storms and flash floods that send walls of water rampaging down the slopes. There could be rock slides, mud or snow avalanches and a dozen other natural disasters that would destroy or injure his sheep. But in spite of such hazards he also knows that this is still the best way to take his flock to the high country.

Phillip Keller

*A Shepherd Looks at Psalm 23*

### *Responding* to the Word

You, O God, are the Lord of the mountains and the valleys. As I travel over mountains and through valleys, I am beneath your feet. You surround me with every kind of creature. Peacocks, pheasants, and wild boars cross my path. Open my eyes to see their beauty, that I may perceive them as the work of your hands.

In your power, in your thought, all things are abundant.

Tonight I will sleep beneath your feet, O Lord of the mountains and valleys, ruler of the trees and vines. I will rest in your love, with you protecting me as a father protects his children, with you watching over me as a mother watches over her children. Then tomorrow the sun will rise and I will not know where I am; but I know that you will guide my footsteps.

Robert Van de Weyer

*Book of Prayers*

### *Reading* the Word

As the deer pants for streams of water,
so my soul pants for you, O God.
My soul thirsts for God, for the living God.
*(Psalm 42:1-2, NIV)*

### *Reflecting* on the Word

Our longings for God may not be as ravenous as David's, but they are as real. Because the hunger hurts, though, we try to take the edge off it in any way we can. One of those ways is with religious activity. And that can include the activity of reading books, listening to tapes, or going to seminars. Through these things, which are often very good things, even nourishing things, we are fed the experiences of others. But they are not our experiences. I can read a psalm about David crying out from a cave in the wilderness, and I should read that psalm, but it is not my psalm. It is not my psalm because it is not my cave, not my wilderness, and not my tears.

For so long in my life I expected my experience of God to be like one of those psalms, structured with pleasing rhythms, full of poetic images, a thing of beauty and grace. What I learned is that those psalms were borne out of great hunger—a hunger that no food on this earth can satisfy.

"He who is satisfied has never truly craved," said Abraham Heschel, and he said this, I think, because he knew

38

that heaven's richest food does not satisfy our longings but rather intensifies them.

Ken Gire
*Windows of the Soul*

### *Responding* to the Word

O God, I have tasted Thy goodness, and it has both satisfied me and made me thirsty for more. I am painfully conscious of my need of further grace. I am ashamed of my lack of desire. O God, the Triune God, I want to want Thee; I long to be filled with longing; I thirst to be made more thirsty still.

A.W. Tozer
*The Pursuit of God*

39

### *Reading* the Word

Cease striving and know that I am God. *(Psalm 46:10)*

### *Reflecting* on the Word

The call to be still, to stand silent, to cease striving, comes in the context of a life in chaos. A life surrounded by land slides, tidal waves, and earthquakes. Whether the chaos is environmental, political, relational, emotional, or simply organizational, there is a river, the psalmist tells us, that flows from the throne of God. A river that remains clear and refreshing, undisturbed by the upheavals. A river whose streams bring gladness. The gladness we can have in the midst of turbulent times, the peace that flows like a river, is the nearness of our God.

"The Lord of hosts is with us," the psalmist assures us.

"The God of Jacob is our stronghold."

He is with us when our world caves in around us.

When the marriage others looked up to slips into the heart of the sea. When once-calm relationships now roar and foam.

When the once-stable mountain of financial security now quakes.

He is "our refuge and strength."

"A very present help in trouble."

We will never know it, though, unless we cease striving and still our heart.

Ken Gire

### *Responding* to the Word

Lord, I feel like a mouse in a treadmill.

Rushing around, faster and faster.

Getting nowhere.

And the first thing that goes out of the window is you.

No time, Lord, sorry!

Then my family.

They should know I'm busy and not ask for my time!

And my friends.

Can't they see all the things I have to do?

Lord, it's at times like this that I need you most.

Yet you seem so far away.

Why, Lord? Where have you gone?

Then I hear it, the quiet voice . . .

. . . be still and know that I am God.

You are near. You have been all the time.

And I understand that I can't hear you if I don't give time to you.

Lord, I just thought so much depended on me. I know the whole world wouldn't end if I took a break, but it made me feel important. I need to remember that it's your world, your work. I'm glad to have a part in it, but it's yours, not mine. And when I've done what I can, I can safely leave the rest to you.

Eddie Askew

*A Silence and a Shouting*

### *Reading* the Word

Make me to hear joy and gladness,
Let the bones which Thou has broken rejoice. *(Psalm 51:8)*

### *Reflecting* on the Word

Occasionally a sheep will develop a habit of going astray. Every evening when the shepherd counts the flock he finds the same sheep missing. Night after night, he goes out seeking the lost animal. After this has occurred several times, the shepherd will once more go out to find the sheep, but this time before carrying it back to the fold, he will break its leg. Back in the fold the shepherd makes a splint for the shattered leg and, during the days that follow, he carries that crippled sheep close to his heart. As the leg begins to mend, the shepherd sets the sheep down by his side. To the crippled animal, the smallest stream looms like a giant river, the tiniest knoll rises like a mountain. The sheep depends completely on the shepherd to carry it across the terrain. After the leg has healed the sheep has learned a lesson: It must stay close to the shepherd's side.

Many feel that it is an act of cruelty for a shepherd to break the leg of a poor, defenseless sheep. It seems hardhearted, almost vicious, until you understand the shepherd's heart. Then you realize that what seems to be cruelty is really kindness. The shepherd knows that the sheep must remain close to him if it is to be protected from danger. So he breaks its leg, not to hurt it, but to restore it.

Haddon Robinson
*Psalm Twenty-three*

### *Responding* to the Word

Lord You know I'm such a stupid sheep.
I worry about all sorts of things
whether I'll find grazing land
still cool water
a fold at night
in which I can feel safe.
I don't.
I only find troubles, want, loss.
I turn aside from You to plan my rebel way.
I go astray.
I follow other shepherds
even other stupid sheep.
Then when I end up on some dark mountain
cliffs before, wild animals behind
I start to bleat Shepherd Shepherd
find me save me or I die.
And You do.

Joseph Bayly
*Psalms of My Life*

## *Reading* the Word

Just as a father has compassion on his children,
So the Lord has compassion on those who fear Him.
*(Psalm 103:13)*

## *Reflecting* on the Word

God loves us as a "Father." And I wondered why He does. What would this kind of love be like from His perspective. A scene flashed onto the wall of my memory.

It was in the middle of a winter night some years back, shortly after I had seriously tried to give God the key to my future. One of our children had called out in the darkness, "Daaady!" I was surprised since they usually called their mother. But I got up, stumbled into her room and carried her into the bathroom. . . . Her head lolled gently to one side and then she would catch herself, but never quite awaken. As I stood there looking at the softness of her face with her eyes closed, and the slightly tousled long blond hair, I was filled with the most amazing sense of love and gratitude to God for that little girl. I kissed her gently on the nose and thought, "Some day you and I will remember this as a time of great closeness." And I could picture us talking about that night when she was a grown girl. But then I realized that she would never remember this midnight closeness——because she had been asleep the whole time I was holding her. But even though she was asleep and would not remem-

44

ber these moments, my own love for her had in some way filled and changed my life as I had quietly helped her through a long winter night.

As I tucked her back in bed with a kiss, it struck me that in some sense this might be one of the reasons the whole Christian venture is worth it to God, in light of our amazing lack of awareness of His presence. I saw that He has been with me all along, loving me and helping me in the most mundane ways, even during those long nights of doubt when I have been spiritually asleep, oblivious to His presence. But even then, when I might least have been trying to respond to Him, His love for me may in some way have warmed His life . . . as my love for my little girl did mine.

Keith Miller

*Habitation of Dragons*

45

### *Responding* to the Word

Lord, thank You that while we were yet sinners, while we were asleep to the fact that You were even interested in us, You loved us enough to die for us in Christ. Help us to be able to love those people in our world who cannot respond to others because they are still asleep to the meaning of the kind of love You have given us to pass on.

Keith Miller

*Habitation of Dragons*

## *Reading* the Word

What shall I render to the Lord
For all His benefits toward me?
I shall lift up the cup of salvation,
And call upon the name of the Lord.
I shall pay my vows to the Lord,
Oh may it be in the presence of all His people.
Precious in the sight of the Lord
Is the death of His godly ones.
O Lord, surely I am Thy servant,
I am Thy servant, the son of Thy handmaid,
Thou hast loosed my bonds.
To Thee I shall offer a sacrifice of thanksgiving.
*(Psalm 116:12-17a)*

## *Reflecting* on the Word

A thankful life is a response to seeing life as a gift from God and realizing that our lives belong to God. God is the Giver; we are thanks-givers.

But to recognize the gifts and the Giver we need to be alert and awake; to have our eyes, ears, minds, and hearts open to what is going on around us. We need to savor each moment as

46

though it were a bowl of homemade soup prepared by someone who loves us very much.

Don Postema
*Space for God*

### *Responding* to the Word

Lord, may your kingdom come into my heart to sanctify me, nourish me and purify me. How insignificant is the passing moment to the eye without faith! But how important each moment is to the eye enlightened by faith! How can we deem insignificant anything which has been caused by you? Every moment and every event is guided by you, and so contains your infinite greatness.

So, Lord, I glorify you in everything that happens to me. In whatever manner you make me live and die, I am content. Events please me for their own sake, regardless of their consequences, because your action lies behind them. Everything is heaven to me, because all my moments manifest your love.

Jean-Pierre De Caussade
*Book of Prayers*
compiled by Robert Van de Weyer

## *Reading* the Word

My frame was not hidden from Thee,
When I was made in secret. . . .
Thine eyes have seen my unformed substance;
And in Thy book they were all written,
The days that were ordained for me
When as yet there was not one of them. *(Psalm 139:15-16)*

## *Reflecting* on the Word

48 They say it's good for one who has lost a loved one to peer into the casket, even just briefly. The casket lies open to help the living close the lid on their relationship with the one who died, to help them accept with their hearts what they know in their minds—that the life in their loved one is gone.

With an early miscarriage there is no funeral, no viewing, no visual aid to bring closure to the heart.

We know nothing about our baby. We have no memories to help us mourn. There's nothing to let go of because there was nothing to hold on to, except a dream. There were no features that we had fallen in love with, no fingers that tapered like his dad's, no smile like his grandma's. No endearing ways about him, all his own. No laugh to ring in our minds when we think of him. Not even a memory of hearing his heart flutter through the doppler; he died too young.

We don't know anything about him, except that he was loved.

Julie Martin
*A Time to Be Born*

### *Responding* to the Word

one day we will join you at the Table
and you will tell us about your life with Jesus
about the gift of love He's given you
that will never be broken or lost

so although we will never scoot you up to our table
teach you how to blow out your candles
wipe the frosting from your face
or give you stuffed tokens
of our love
today in our hearts we will sing with the angels
happy birthday to you, dear baby
happy birthday to you

Julie Martin
*A Time to Be Born*

49

### *Reading* the Word

Sing to the Lord with thanksgiving;
Sing praises to our God on the lyre,
Who covers the heavens with clouds,
Who provides rain for the earth,
Who makes grass to grow on the mountains.
He gives to the beast its food,
And to the young ravens which cry. . . .
He satisfies you with the finest of wheat. *(Psalm 147:7-9, 14)*

50

### *Reflecting* on the Word

Though every good gift comes from God, most of those gifts pass through so many hands that by the time we get them we often miss seeing His hand in the giving.

Take, for example, the orange juice you maybe drank this morning. It came out of a carton in your refrigerator. The carton was sold to you by a grocer. It was transported to the grocery store by a trucker. The orange juice was packaged in a plant by a manufacturer, where the oranges were probably also squeezed. The oranges were shipped there by another trucker, whose truck was probably loaded by migrant workers, who picked the oranges from the groves. The groves were owned by a farmer, whose harvest depended on just the right amounts of sunshine and rain and good weather. All of which originate from the hand of God.

Every good thing that comes to us in life can be traced back to that hand.

It seems the least we can do with each of those good things is to thank Him.

Ken Gire

### *Responding* to the Word

For flowers, for seashells,
for art, for music,
for birds, for dogs,
for ducks, for geese,
for water, for air,
for sky, for stars,
for sunshine, for earth,
for grass, for food,
for drink, for laughter,
for affection, for my friends,
for my family, for my parents,
for my children, for my beloved husband,
for my life,
thank you, God . . . even if it's all only a loan.

Joan Bel Geddes<br>*Are You Listening God?*

51

### *Reading* the Word

A good man is concerned for the welfare of his animals. . . .
*(Proverbs 12:10, TLB)*

### *Reflecting* on the Word

As far back as I can remember I was saddened by the amount of misery I saw in the world around me. . . .

One thing that especially saddened me was that unfortunate animals had to suffer so much pain and misery. The sight of an old limping horse, tugged forward by one man while another kept beating it with a stick to get it to the knacker's yard at Colmar, haunted me for weeks.

It was quite incomprehensible to me why in my evening prayers I should pray for human beings only. So when my mother had prayed with me and kissed me good night, I used to add silently a prayer that I had composed myself for all living creatures.

Albert Schweitzer
*Reverence for Life*

### *Responding* to the Word

[The prayer] ran thus: "O, heavenly Father, protect and bless all things that have breath; guard them from all evil, and let them sleep in peace."

Albert Schweitzer
*Reverence for Life*

### *Reading* the Word

Remember also your Creator in the days of your youth, before the evil days come and the years draw near when you will say, "I have no delight in them"; before the sun, the light, the moon, and the stars are darkened, and clouds return after the rain; in the day that the watchmen of the house tremble, and mighty men stoop, the grinding ones stand idle because they are few, and those who look through windows grow dim; and the doors on the street are shut as the sound of the grinding mill is low, and one will arise at the sound of the bird and all the daughters of song will sing softly. . . . Remember Him before the silver cord is broken and the golden bowl is crushed, the pitcher by the well is shattered and the wheel at the cistern is crushed; then the dust will return to the earth as it was, and the spirit will return to God who gave it. *(Ecclesiastes 12:1-4, 6-7)*

### *Reflecting* on the Word

I am progressing along the path of life in my ordinary content-edly fallen and godless condition, absorbed in a merry meeting with my friends for the morrow or a bit of work that tickles my vanity to-day, a holiday or a new book, when suddenly a stab of abdominal pain that threatens serious disease, or a headline in the newspapers that threatens us all with destruction, sends this whole pack of cards tumbling down. At first I am overwhelmed, and all my little happinesses look like broken toys. Then, slowly

54

and reluctantly, bit by bit, I try to bring myself into the frame of mind that I should be in at all times. I remind myself that all these toys were never intended to possess my heart, that my true good is in another world and my only real treasure is Christ.

C.S. Lewis
*The Problem of Pain*

### *Responding* to the Word

Dear Lord, thank You for the signposts of physical change and death which force me to see the frail and transient nature of my life without You. I pray that in times of health and success I will not forget You and turn away. Give me the courage to face the stark realities of life and help me to move through each stage of development with a perspective of wisdom and joy instead of fear, knowing that You will be with me.

Keith Miller
*Habitation of Dragons*

### *Reading* the Word

My beloved responded and said to me,
"Arise, my darling, my beautiful one,
And come along."
For behold, the winter is past,
The rain is over and gone.
The flowers have already appeared in the land;
The time has arrived for pruning the vines,
And the voice of the turtledove has been heard in our land.
The fig tree has ripened its figs,
And the vines in blossom have given forth their fragrance.
"Arise, my darling, my beautiful one,
And come along!" *(Song of Solomon 2:10-13)*

### *Reflecting* on the Word

Have you ever wondered why spring has always been the season for lovers, the background of romantic literature in every century? It must be because the season of spring reflects the experience of the young lovers. Everything is fresh; new life flows through the world; happiness and colors triumph over winter's boring grays. Whenever any couple falls in love, it is spring for them because their lives are fresh; everything in life has a new perspective; what was black and white is now in color; what was dark is light. . . .

New love brings new life. Spring lovers, like spring trees, though plain and barren in winter, become full and lovely in spring.

One good indication of real love is the desire to communicate, a wish to discover all about this person whom you love so much. No detail seems too trivial to be related. No mood or feeling of one is unimportant to the other. And you care about the details and the feelings because you care so much about the person.

S. Craig Glickman
*A Song for Lovers*

### *Responding* to the Word

Show me Thy glory, I pray Thee, that so I may know Thee indeed. Begin in mercy a new work of love within me. Say to my soul, "Rise up, my love, my fair one, and come away." Then give me grace to rise and follow Thee up from this misty lowland where I have wandered so long. In Jesus' name. Amen.

A.W. Tozer
*The Pursuit of God*

### *Reading* the Word

Can a woman forget her nursing child,
And have no compassion on the son of her womb?
Even these may forget, but I will not forget you. *(Isaiah 49:15)*

### *Reflecting* on the Word

Asleep, until your delicate cry cracks open an eyelid of the night.
It's feeding time, for both of us. I stroke your warm head, nurse
your drowsy body. And you, tiny hand on my breast, you nourish my soul. Although day is dawning somewhere across the
globe, to me the whole world is you and me, the dim lamp in
the corner, and the moon.

Julie Martin
*A Time to Be Born*

### *Responding* to the Word

Lord, as I hold her in my arms and kiss her tiny fingers
I wonder if anyone in all the world
Has ever been as happy as I am now!
She's like a tiny poem
Short but beautiful—
And several years from now she'll be a story.
Lord, I'm trusting you to write the plot.
Then at last she'll be a book-length novel

Translated into many languages.
I am confident of this, Lord
For you are both Author and Publisher.

Ruth Harms Calkin
*Life's Little Prayer Book*
compiled by Gary Lahoda

### *Reading* the Word

Can a woman forget her nursing child,
And have no compassion on the son of her womb?
*(Isaiah 49:15a)*

Hear my cry, O God. . . . *(Psalm 61:1a)*

### *Reflecting* on the Word

A mother's body responds to her child's cry even before her
brain has had time to think about it. Her breast has many little
ducts and channels which are full of milk. These ducts have a
smooth muscle around them which is relaxed until she hears the
baby's cry. Then the muscle involuntarily contracts. When the
baby's lips touch the nipple even more contraction is stimulat-
ed. Sometimes the cry itself is enough to result in a little fountain of milk squirting from a duct. It's as if the breast were in as
much of a hurry to supply the milk as the baby is to receive it!

Paul Brand

*The Forever Feast*

### *Responding* to the Word

Dear Lord,

Thank you that you have stooped to use the quiet, gentle image
of a mother nursing her baby to describe the feelings you have
for your children. That one image communicates so much to

me, for I know even now that there is no way I could ever forget this baby who will nurse at my breast. My compassion flows out to him as freely as the milk from my breast. And if that's true, Lord, how much more does the milk of divine compassion flow out for your children. Especially when they cry out in the middle of the night, pierced with hunger, alone and scared and shivering in the dark.

Lord, when I cry out to you in my emptiness, help me to realize that you have not forgotten me; when I cry out in my aloneness, help me to understand that you have not forsaken me. Through my tears, help me to see that you are there, aching with maternal feelings, longing to take me in your arms where the milk of your compassion will be my food; the softness of your breast, my pillow; and the rhythms of your heart, the lullaby that sings me to sleep.

It is such a beautiful image you have chosen, Lord. Bring it to mind every time I nurse. And keep it in my mind all the days of my life. For one day I too may be shivering in the dark, feeling empty and alone, and desperately needing the comfort of your breast. . . .

Mary C. Wells and Judy Gire

Robert G. Wells, M.D., and Ken Gire

*Miracle of Life*

61

## *Reading* the Word

The word which came to Jeremiah from the Lord saying, "Arise and go down to the potter's house, and there I shall announce My words to you." Then I went down to the potter's house, and there he was, making something on the wheel. But the vessel that he was making of clay was spoiled in the hand of the potter; so he remade it into another vessel, as it pleased the potter to make.

Then the word of the Lord came to me saying, "Can I not, O house of Israel, deal with you as this potter does?" declares the Lord. "Behold, like the clay in the potter's hand, so are you in My hand, O house of Israel. *(Jeremiah 18:1-6)*

## *Reflecting* on the Word

As our prayer life matures, we become more and more aware of being the clay in the hands of the potter. The clay can do virtually nothing to transform itself into an object of beauty. But it can be soft, pliable, sensitive to the potter's touch. People often talk about their fear that God's will may break them, that what he asks is too hard for them to bear. And yet the clay is never broken by anything the potter may do to it——unless the clay has become hard and rigid. As long as it is malleable it will never break, but once it begins to resist the potter's touch, to push against his shaping, it will be very much in danger of breaking. This is what happened to Israel, and that is why Yahweh sent Jeremiah to tell her that she needed to be broken in order to be refashioned according to the potter's design. Even her breaking was not to be for her destruction but for her healing.

So it is with us.

Thomas H. Green, S. J.
*When the Well Runs Dry*

### *Responding* to the Word

Have Thine own way, Lord!
Have Thine own way!
Thou art the Potter;
I am the clay.
Mould me and make me.
After Thy will,
While I am waiting,
Yielded and still.

63

George C. Stebbins
A. A. P.
*Have Thine Own Way, Lord*

## *Reading* the Word

The Lord is good to those who wait for Him,
To the person who seeks Him.
It is good that he waits silently
For the salvation of the Lord. *(Lamentations 3:25-26)*

## *Reflecting* on the Word

Waiting is not simply another religious activity to be added to the rest. Though we have methods to help us—meditation and silence, for example—waiting is more than physical silence. It is a movement of the heart, a stance we take before God. Waiting is an inner acquiescence, releasing our striving and abandoning our lives entirely to the work of God. Quieting our whole selves, we surrender our activity, our plans, and our dreams. When we wait, we yield up our expectations of what God should do, our precious hoards of ritual and doctrine, our social awareness, and our self-concepts. Waiting is totally submitting to God and inviting God to move in our hearts with complete freedom.

Howard Macy
*Rhythms of the Inner Life*

64

## *Responding* to the Word

O Lord God,
great distress has come upon me;
my cares threaten to crush me,
and I do not know what to do.
O God, be gracious to me and help me.
Give me the strength to bear what you send,
and do not let fear rule over me;
Take a father's care of my wife and children.

O merciful God,
forgive me all the sins that I have committed
against you and against my fellow men.
I trust in your grace
and commit my life wholly in your hands.
Do with me according to your will
and as is best for me.
Whether I live or whether I die, I am with you,
and you, my God, are with me,
Lord, I wait for your salvation,
and for your Kingdom.
Amen.

65

Dietrich Bonhoeffer
*Letters and Papers from Prison*
(written Christmas, 1943, in a Nazi concentration camp)

### *Reading* the Word

And the Lord appointed a great fish to swallow Jonah, and
Jonah was in the stomach of the fish three days and three nights.
Then Jonah prayed to the Lord from the stomach of the fish,
and he said, "I called out of my distress to the Lord,
And He answered me.
I cried for help from the depth of Sheol;
Thou didst hear my voice.
For Thou hadst cast me into the deep,
Into the heart of the seas,
And the current engulfed me.
All Thy breakers and billows passed over me." *(Jonah 1:17-2:3)*

### *Reflecting* on the Word

We become what we are called to be by praying. And we start
out by praying from the belly of the fish.

The belly of the fish is a place of confinement, a tight,
restricted place. The ship to Tarshish was headed for the western horizon—limitless expanses of sea with the lure of the mysterious and beckoning unknown through the Straits of
Gibraltar and beyond. The Gates of Hercules. Atlantis.
Hesperides. Ultima Thule.

Religion always plays on these sublime aspirations, these
erotic drives for completion and wholeness. Jonah, heady with
this potent elixir and cruising confidently under full sails, the sea

breeze and salt tang deepening the sensory anticipation of a thrilling life in the service of God, found himself instead in the belly of the fish . . . the unattractive opposite to everything Jonah had set out for.

Eugene Peterson
*Under the Unpredictable Plant*

### *Responding* to the Word

My prayers, God, flow from what I am not;
I think thy answers make me what I am.
Like weary waves thought flows upon thought,
But the still depth beneath is all thine own,
And there thou mov'st in paths to us unknown.
Out of the strange strife thy peace is strangely wrought;
If the lion in us pray—thou answerest the lamb.

George MacDonald

### *Reading* the Word

An angel of the Lord appeared to him in a dream, saying, "Joseph, son of David, do not be afraid to take Mary as your wife; for that which has been conceived in her is of the Holy Spirit. And she will bear a Son; and you shall call His name Jesus, for it is He who will save His people from their sins." Now all this took place that what was spoken by the Lord through the prophet might be fulfilled, saying, "Behold, the virgin shall be with child, and shall bear a Son, and they shall call His name Immanuel," which translated means, "God with us." *(Matthew 1:20-23)*

68

### *Reflecting* on the Word

The implications of the name Immanuel are both comforting and unsettling. Comforting, because He has come to share the danger as well as the drudgery of our everyday lives. He desires to weep with us and to wipe away our tears. And what seems most bizarre, Jesus Christ, the Son of God, longs to share in and to be the source of the laughter and the joy we all too rarely know.

The implications are unsettling. It is one thing to claim that God looks down upon us, from a safe distance, and speaks to us (via long distance, we hope). But to say that He is right here, is to put ourselves and Him in a totally new situation. He is no longer the calm and benevolent observer in the sky, the kindly old caricature with the beard. His image becomes that of Jesus, who wept and laughed, who fasted and feasted, and who, above all, was fully present to those He loved. He was there with them. He is here with us. . . .

He is with us in the midst of our daily, routine lives. In the middle of cleaning the house or driving somewhere in the pickup. . . . Often it's in the middle of the most mundane task that He lets us know He is there with us. We realize, then, that there can be no "ordinary" moments for people who live their lives with Jesus.

Michael Card

*The Name of the Promise Is Jesus*

### *Responding* to the Word 69

You speak, Lord, to all men in general through general events. Revolutions are simply the tides of your Providence, which stir up storms and tempests in people's minds. You speak to men in particular through particular events, as they occur moment by moment. But instead of hearing your voice, instead of respecting events as signals of your loving guidance, people see nothing else but blind chance and human decision. They find objections to everything you say. They wish to add to or subtract from your Word. They wish to change and reform it.

Teach me, dear Lord, to read clearly this book of life. I wish to be like a simple child, accepting your word regardless of whether I understand your purposes. It is enough for me that you speak.

Jean-Pierre De Caussade

### *Reading* the Word

Then Jesus was led up by the Spirit into the wilderness to be tempted by the devil. And after He had fasted forty days and forty nights, He then became hungry. And the tempter came and said to Him, "If You are the Son of God, command these stones to become bread." But He answered and said, "It is written, 'Man shall not live on bread alone, but on every word that proceeds out of the mouth of God.'" *(Matthew 4:1-4)*

### *Reflecting* on the Word

70

Wormwood to his demonic apprentice: Sooner or later [God] withdraws, if not in fact, at least from their conscious experience, all those supports and incentives. He leaves the creature to stand on its own legs—to carry out from the will alone duties which have lost all relish. It is during such trough periods, much more than during the peak periods, that it is growing into the sort of creature He wants it to be. Hence the prayers offered in the state of dryness are those which please Him best. We can drag our patients along by continual tempting, because we design them only for the table, and the more their will is interfered with the better. He cannot "tempt" to virtue as we do to vice. He wants them to learn to walk and must therefore take away His hand; and if only the will to walk is really there He is pleased even with their stumbles.

C.S. Lewis
*The Screwtape Letters*

### *Responding* to the Word

O God, there are things about which I can't talk to anyone except you. There are things in me about which no one knows except myself and you.

The things which I should not even want fascinate me. The thoughts which I should never allow into my mind, I cannot keep out.

So far I have resisted wrong things, but I know my own weakness, and I am afraid of myself.

O God, come to me with your cleansing power, and make me able to overcome evil and to do the right.

I ask even more—fill me with such a love of you that I will not even want to sin anymore.

This I ask for Jesus' sake. Amen.

William Barclay
*A Guide to Daily Prayer*

## *Reading* the Word

Blessed are the poor in spirit, for theirs is
    the kingdom of heaven.
Blessed are those who mourn, for they
    shall be comforted.
Blessed are the gentle, for they shall inherit the earth.
Blessed are those who hunger and thirst for righteousness,
for they shall be satisfied.
Blessed are the merciful, for they shall receive mercy.
Blessed are the pure in heart, for they shall see God.
Blessed are the peacemakers, for they shall be called
    the sons of God.
Blessed are those who have been persecuted for the
    sake of righteousness,
    for theirs is the kingdom of heaven.
Blessed are you when men casts insults at you, and persecute
you, and say all kinds of evil against you falsely, on account of
Me. Rejoice, and be glad, for your reward in heaven is great, for
so they persecuted the prophets who were before you.
*(Matthew 5:3-12)*

## *Reflecting* on the Word

On the first reading of the Sermon on the Mount you feel it
turns everything upside down, but the second time you read it,
you discover that it turns everything right side up. The first time

you read it you feel that it is impossible, but the second time, you feel that nothing else is possible.

G.K. Chesterton

### *Responding* to the Word

Lord, make me an instrument of thy peace;
where there is hatred, let me sow love;
where there is injury, pardon;
where there is doubt, faith;
where there is despair, hope;
where there is darkness, light;
and where there is sadness, joy.
O Divine Master,
grant that I may not so much seek
to be consoled as to console;
to be understood, as to understand;
to be loved, as to love;
for it is in giving that we receive,
it is in pardoning that we are pardoned,
and it is in dying that we are born to eternal life.

St. Francis of Assisi

73

### *Reading* the Word

Blessed are those who mourn, for they shall be comforted.
*(Matthew 5:4)*

### *Reflecting* on the Word

Look back at those hours which passed over your life so calmly and contentedly. . . . If the whole of your life had been a succession of hours like those, do you know what would have become of you? You would become selfish, hardhearted, lonely, without regard for higher things, for the pure, for God—and you would never have felt blessedness. When did it first dawn on you that we men don't live unto ourselves? When did the blessedness of compassion bring comfort to you? In suffering. Where did your heart come close to those who were so distant and cold to you? In suffering. Where did you catch a glimpse of the higher destiny of your life? In suffering. Where did you feel God was near to you? In suffering. Where did you first realize the blessedness of having a Father in heaven? In suffering.

Albert Schweitzer
*Reverence for Life*

### *Responding* to the Word

Dear Jesus,
Thank you for the hard and sometimes uphill road I have had

74

to walk in following you. I am stronger because of it. And we are closer because of it. For all the good things that have come to me along the way, I thank you.

But I have to say, I wish it were an easier way,

a shorter way,

a more scenic way.

I wish the road didn't have to go past the garden of Gethsemane, with its darkness and loneliness and tears.

I wish it just went in endless circles around the seashores of Galilee, and that walking with you were more of a serene stroll in the sunset.

Help me to understand that Gethsemane is as necessary as Galilee in the geography of a growing soul.

Help me to remember that even though you were a son, yet you learned obedience through the things you suffered.

Paul talks about entering into the fellowship of your suffering. I do so very much look forward to having fellowship with you, but honestly, Lord, the thought of having to suffer to experience it stops me in my tracks.

Help me, Lord Jesus, to want your company more than I want serenity, and to love the fellowship with you more than I fear the suffering necessary to enter into it.

Ken Gire

## *Reading* the Word

You have heard that the ancients were told, "You shall not commit murder" and "Whoever commits murder shall be liable to the court." But I say to you that everyone who is angry with his brother shall be guilty. . . . *(Matthew 5:21-22)*

## *Reflecting* on the Word

Anger is always an attack on the brother's life, for it refuses to let him live and aims at his destruction. Jesus will not accept the common distinction between righteous indignation and unjustifiable anger. The disciple must be entirely innocent of anger, because anger is an offence against both God and his neighbour. Every idle word which we think so little of betrays our lack of respect for our neighbour, and shows that we place ourselves on a pinnacle above him and value our own lives higher than his. The angry word is a blow struck at our brother, a stab at his heart: it seeks to hit, to hurt and to destroy. A deliberate insult is even worse, for we are then openly disgracing our brother in the eyes of the world, and causing others to despise him. With our hearts burning with hatred, we seek to annihilate his moral and material existence. We are passing judgement on him, and that is murder. And the murderer will himself be judged.

Dietrich Bonhoeffer
*The Cost of Discipleship*

### *Responding* to the Word

Father, Thou knowest the misunderstanding that has risen between me and my friend. Harsh and thoughtless words have been spoken. I know that this rift grieves Thee, that Thou wouldst be far more impressed with a sacrifice of reconciliation on my part than with any vows of loyalty or material gift I could make Thee.

I dare not make this a prayer for Thee to change _____; my friend is Thy responsibility. I know that always I must begin with my responsibility—myself and my own shortcomings. . . .

Enable me now to let all false pride go. Give me the courage that will enable me to go to _____ and be the first to say, "I have been wrong here and here. I am sorry. Forgive me."

Help me not to take myself too seriously. Grant to me objectivity and a quiet mind and a sense of humor.

Go Thou ahead of me to fling out a bridge of good will, to cast down all roadblocks of misunderstanding. And bless to Thy glory and the happiness of all concerned this gesture of good will undertaken in Thy name. Amen.

Peter Marshall

### *Reading* the Word

You have heard that it was said, "You shall love your neighbor, and hate your enemy." But I say to you, love your enemies, and pray for those who persecute you in order that you may be sons of your Father who is in heaven; for He causes His sun to rise on the evil and the good, and sends rain on the righteous and the unrighteous. *(Matthew 5:43-45)*

### *Reflecting* on the Word

78 Returning hate for hate multiplies hate, adding deeper darkness to a night already devoid of stars. Darkness cannot drive out darkness; only light can do that. Hate cannot drive out hate; only love can do that. Hate multiplies hate, violence multiplies violence, and toughness multiplies toughness in a descending spiral of destruction. So when Jesus says "Love your enemies," he is setting forth a profound and ultimately inescapable admonition. Have we not come to such an impasse in the modern world that we must love our enemies—or else? The chain reaction of evil—hate begetting hate, wars producing more wars—must be broken, or we shall be plunged into the dark abyss of annihilation.

Martin Luther King, Jr.
*Strength to Love*

## *Responding* to the Word

*(During World War II, ninety-two thousand women and children died at the death camp Ravensbruck. Most of them were Jews. This prayer was found scrawled on a scrap of paper near a dead child.)*

Lord, remember not only the men and women of good will but also those of ill will. But do not only remember the suffering they have inflicted on us; remember the fruits we have brought, thanks to this suffering—our comradeship, our loyalty, our humility, the courage, the generosity, the greatness of heart which has grown out of all this, and when they come to judgment, let all the fruits we have borne be their forgiveness.

## *Reading* the Word

Do not lay up for yourselves treasures upon earth, where moth and rust destroy, and where thieves break in and steal. But lay up for yourselves treasures in heaven, where neither moth nor rust destroys, and where thieves do not break in or steal; for where your treasure is, there will your heart be also.
*(Matthew 6:19-21)*

## *Reflecting* on the Word

80   People are very interested in and think about their treasures. If you have bought investments, lands, houses, you have an interest in that particular part of the world, wherever it may be. If you have given money to people for the Lord's work, those people and that work take up part of your interest, your "heart" and then, because it is also a treasure in heaven, your thoughts are concerned more about the things the Lord tells us of heaven, than if everything had been "invested" here on earth. You can't grow spiritually if your thoughts are always on earthly investments. It makes a difference to your spiritual growth when you are laying up treasure in heaven. It makes heaven more like a home you are preparing to move into.

Edith Schaeffer
*Everybody Can Know*

### *Responding* to the Word

Lord, God,

I am possessed by legions of things, even as the
Gadarene was possessed.

I speak of my things as possessions—but it is I who
am possessed.

I am fettered, bound to routine and structured days—
by the tyranny of things.

I ought to visit the sick, but I haven't finished dusting
the knickknacks.

I need to feed the hungry, but I've got to stay home
and water the grass.

The naked are waiting to be clothed, but I've got to take
the stereo to the shop.

I have allowed my life to become so cluttered with possessions
that I am rendered ineffective. I forget about people. I don't
have time to be bothered with them. Gradually, insidiously,
things have become the possessor, and I the possessed.

It is not that material possessions in themselves are bad.
They can be tools, enabling me to do what I really need to do.
But my priorities are misplaced when I focus on the things
themselves, and not on what they can enable me to do.

Dear Lord, deliver me from the tyranny of things.

Restore my perspective—thy perspective. Amen.

Jo Carr and Imogene Sorley
*Plum Jelly & Stained Glass*

81

### *Reading* the Word

"Look at the birds, free and unfettered, not tied down to a job description, careless in the care of God. And you count far more to him than birds." *(Matthew 6:26, TM)*

### *Reflecting* on the Word

*Careless in the care of God.* And why shouldn't they be?
For their food, He provides insects in the air,
    seeds on the ground.
For their search for food, He provides eyes that are keen,
    wings that are swift.
For their drinking, He provides poolings of rainwater.
For their bathing, He provides puddles.
For their survival, He provides migratory instincts to take
    them to warmer climates.
For their flight, He provides bones that are porous and
    lightweight.
For their warmth, He provides feathers.
For their dryness, He provides a water-resistant coating.
For their rest, He provides warm updrafts so they
    can glide through the air.
For their journey, He provides the company of other travelers.
For their return, He provides the companionship of a mate.
For their safety, He provides a perch in branches far
    from the reach of predators.

For their nest, He provides twigs.

And for every newborn beak, He provides enough worms so they can grow up to leave the nest and continue the cycle of life.

It's no wonder they're so free from the cares of this world.

The wonder is, if we count more to Him than birds, why aren't we?

Ken Gire

### *Responding* to the Word

Grant unto us, almighty God,
the peace of God that passeth understanding,
That we, amid the storms and troubles of this our life,
may rest in thee, knowing that all things are in thee;
Not beneath thine eye only, but under thy care,
governed by thy will, guarded by thy love,
So that with a quiet heart we may see the storms of life,
the cloud and the thick darkness,
Ever rejoicing to know that the darkness and the light
are both alike to thee. . . .

George Dawson

83

### *Reading* the Word

Therefore, however you want people to treat you, so treat them, for this is the Law and the Prophets. (*Matthew 7:12*)

### *Reflecting* on the Word

We hesitate to be the first to apply the Golden Rule; we feel that it isn't safe, that we must wait until the whole world is ready to apply it with us. But that is why the whole world never is ready—they're all leaving it to the other fellow to start. Of course it isn't safe. We shall lose many worldly advantages if we love our neighbors as ourselves; we may even lose our lives. But then, that is what we were told to do.

Christ never offered us security. He left that to the politicians—Caiaphas probably offered lots of it. Christ told us to expect poverty, humiliation, persecution, and pain, and to know ourselves blessed through accepting them. The good news out of Nazareth was never reassuring news by this world's standards; reassuring news has a way of coming from the devil. For a long time we have been trying to make the best of both worlds, to accept Christianity as an ideal and materialism as a practice, and in consequence we have reached a spiritual bankruptcy. . . .

Joy Davidman
*Smoke on the Mountain*

### *Responding* to the Word

O God, Father of all, help us to forgive others as we would wish them to forgive us. May we try to understand them as we in turn would like to be understood, in the hope that forgiveness will not be in order. May we see with their eyes, think with their minds, feel with their hearts. Then let us ask ourselves whether we should judge them, or judge ourselves and accept them as children, like us, of one heavenly Father.

William Barclay
*One Prayer at a Time*
edited by F. Forrester Church
and Terrence J. Mulry

85

### *Reading* the Word

Enter by the narrow gate; for the gate is wide, and the way is broad that leads to destruction, and many are those who enter by it. For the gate is small, and the way is narrow that leads to life, and few are those who find it. *(Matthew 7:13-14)*

### *Reflecting* on the Word

The path of discipleship is narrow, and it is fatally easy to miss one's way and stray from the path, even after years of discipleship. And it is hard to find. On either side of the narrow path deep chasms yawn. To be called to a life of extraordinary quality, to live up to it, and yet to be unconscious of it is indeed a narrow way. To confess and testify to the truth as it is in Jesus, and at the same time to love the enemies of that truth, his enemies and ours, to love them with the infinite love of Jesus Christ, is indeed a narrow way. To believe the promise of Jesus that his followers shall possess the earth, and at the same time to face our enemies unarmed and defenceless, preferring to incur injustice rather than to do wrong ourselves, is indeed a narrow way. To see the weakness and wrong in others, and at the same time refrain from judging them; to deliver the gospel message without casting pearls before swine, is indeed a narrow way. The way is unutterably hard, and at every moment we are in danger of straying from it. If we regard this way as one we follow in obedience to an external command, if we are afraid of ourselves all

86

the time, it is indeed an impossible way. But if we behold Jesus
Christ going on before step by step, we shall not go astray. But
if we worry about the dangers that beset us, if we gaze at the
road instead of at him who goes before, we are already straying
from the path. For he is himself the way, the narrow way and
the strait gate. He, and he alone is our journey's end.

Dietrich Bonhoeffer
*The Cost of Discipleship*

### *Responding* to the Word

Help me to consider Him who has endured such hostility by
sinners against Himself, so that I might not grow weary and lose
heart. Help me keep vivid in my mind the extraordinary life He
lived, His calmness with controversy. His storminess with
hypocrisy. His authority in teaching. His humility in serving.
His quickness with compassion. His slowness with condemna-
tion. His readiness in defending others. His reluctance in
defending Himself. His joy at unexpected faith. His sorrow at
unbelief. His submission to the Father. His resistance to the
Devil. His daring in the way He lived. His dignity in the way
He died.

Thank you, O God, for the steps Jesus left behind, so clear
and distinct and unswerving. And so impossible . . . unless my
eyes are ever and always only on Him.

Ken Gire

## *Reading* the Word

You will know them by their fruits. Grapes are not gathered from thorn bushes, nor figs from thistles, are they? *(Matthew 7:16)*

## *Reflecting* on the Word

If grapes weren't delicious people wouldn't eat them and the seeds would never be spread. Think about it. When we walk along a path, eating grapes, we spit out the seeds. All along beside the path these seeds will germinate and new vines will be born.

88      In the biology of the Christian faith, seeds are wrapped in attractive fruit. If a vine bore only naked seeds, nobody would pick them. Everyone who wants to be a disciple of Jesus Christ is expected to bear fruit. This does not mean that we all have to be successful in bringing many people to the point of decision to become a Christian. It means our lives have to bear the taste, the fragrance, or the nourishment that makes people appreciate what we are and what we have to give. The people we work with, the members of our family or Sunday school class, should sense the pleasure and benefit of being with us. They should know that the flavor of our life comes from our abiding in Jesus Christ.

One day something may trigger the beginning of new life in someone you know who has tasted the flavor of Jesus through contact with you. We may not ever know how or when it happens.

But it will be the germination of a seed that was planted because your own personal life was delicious.

Paul Brand
*The Forever Feast*

### *Responding* to the Word

We give thanks for the harvest of the heart's work;
Seeds of faith planted with faith;
Love nurtured by love;
Courage strengthened by courage.
We give thanks for the fruits of the struggling soul,
The bitter and the sweet;
For that which has grown in adversity
And for that which has flourished in warmth and grace;
For the radiance of the spirit in autumn
And for that which must now fade and die.
We are blessed and give thanks.
Amen.

Michael Leunig
*The Prayer Tree*

89

### *Reading* the Word

And as Jesus passed on from there, He saw a man, called Matthew, sitting in the tax office; and He said to him, "Follow Me!" And he rose, and followed Him. *(Matthew 9:9)*

### *Reflecting* on the Word

All that the voice said was, "Follow me"—no forewarning, no explanation, no attempt to persuade. Come on. This way. I will show you. These are words that do not even need a voice to make them heard. The eyes can speak them or a pair of hands. Even silence will do. But we always answer with our feet. We get up and start following. Or we do not. . . .

Who is this who asks us to follow? We want to know who he is before we follow him, and that is understandable enough except that the truth of the matter is that it is only first by following him that we can begin to find out who he is. You do not come first to understand a person fully and then to love him, but love comes first, and then it is out of the love that understanding is born. And I choose the analogy carefully because it is precisely love that set this whole scene in the tax office on fire; and once we see that, we see that Jesus told Matthew to follow him not just for his own sake but for the sake of Matthew, whom he loved. Faith is the word that describes the direction our feet start moving when we find that we are loved. Faith is

90

stepping out into the unknown with nothing to guide us but a hand just beyond our grasp.

Frederick Buechner
*The Magnificent Defeat*

### *Responding* to the Word

Take my life and let it be
Consecrated, Lord, to Thee;
Take my moments and my days,
Let them flow in ceaseless praise.

Take my will and make it Thine,
It shall be no longer mine;
Take my heart, it is Thine own,
It shall be Thy royal throne.

Take my love, my God, I pour
At Thy feet its treasure store;
Take myself, and I will be
Ever, only, all for Thee.
Amen.

*"Take My Life and Let It Be"*
lyrics by Frances R. Havergal, 1874
music by William H. Havergal, 1869

91

### *Reading* the Word

Nor do men put new wine into old wineskins; otherwise the wineskins burst, and the wine pours out, and the wineskins are ruined; but they put new wine into fresh wineskins, and both are preserved. *(Matthew 9:17)*

### *Reflecting* on the Word

The heady tumult of the new gospel! It would burst the Judaistic wineskin—the New Testament Epistles shake under that agitation! Later it would stretch the old bottle of slavery beyond limits, and spill over the world in a new wine of freedom. Man's ancient concept of womanhood was unable to hold the ferment, and was thrown to the debris of broken systems. The red tide running from the winepress of Calvary is not easily restrained!

Then why try to save the old wineskins? They exist for the wine, and only the wine is precious. In each new generation it must be poured from one perishable vessel to another without the spilling of a drop. The discarded vessel need not be mourned so long as the spontaneous energy of the new life is preserved.

George Buttrick
*The Parables of Jesus*

### *Responding* to the Word

O God, I am so fragile:
my dreams get broken,
my relationships get broken,
my heart gets broken,
my body gets broken.

What can I believe,
except that you will not despise a broken heart,
that old and broken people shall yet dream dreams,
and that the lame shall leap for joy,
the blind see,
the deaf hear.

What can I believe,
except what Jesus taught:
that only what is first broken, like bread,
can be shared;
that only what is broken is open to your entry;
that old wineskins must be ripped open and replaced
if the wine of new life is to expand.

Ted Loder
*Guerrillas of Grace*

## *Reading* the Word

And having summoned His twelve disciples, He gave them authority over unclean spirits, to cast them out, and to heal every kind of disease and every kind of sickness. Now the names of the twelve apostles were these: The first, Simon, who is called Peter, and Andrew his brother; and James the son of Zebedee, and John his brother; Philip and Bartholomew; Thomas and Matthew the tax-gatherer; James the son of Alphaeus, and Thaddaeus; Simon the Zealot, and Judas Iscariot, the one who betrayed Him. *(Matthew 10:1-4)*

94

## *Reflecting* on the Word

What can we take with us on this journey to we do not know where? What we must take is the knowledge of our own unending ambiguous motives. . . .

The voice that we hear over our shoulders never says, "First be sure that your motives are pure and selfless and then follow me." If it did, then we could none of us follow. So when later the voice says, "Take up your cross and follow me," at least part of what is meant by "cross" is our realization that we are seldom less than nine parts fake. Yet our feet can insist on answering him anyway, and on we go, step after step, mile after mile.

Frederick Buechner
*The Magnificent Defeat*

### *Responding* to the Word

Give us the courage to follow You even if it means taking the risk, as You did, of being misunderstood. I want to resist phoniness . . . yet without wallowing in the problems of motivation. It all seems very complex, and sometimes I do not even understand my behavior after the fact. So I am offering myself and my subtly mixed motives to You, asking that You will take me beyond such self-centered preoccupations into Your loving perspective.

Keith Miller
*Habitation of Dragons*

### *Reading* the Word

Come to Me, all who are weary and heavy-laden, and I will give you rest. Take My yoke upon you, and learn from Me, for I am gentle and humble in heart; and you shall find rest for your souls. For My yoke is easy, and My load is light.
*(Matthew 11:28-30)*

### *Reflecting* on the Word

The life I have chosen as wife and mother entrains a whole caravan of complications. . . . It involves food and shelter; meals, planning, marketing, bills, and making the ends meet in a thousand ways. . . . It involves health; doctors, dentists, appointments, medicine, cod-liver oil, vitamins, trips to the drugstore. It involves education, spiritual, intellectual, physical; schools, school conferences, car-pools, extra trips for basketball or orchestra practice. . . . It involves clothes, shopping, laundry, cleaning, mending, letting skirts down and sewing buttons on. . . . It involves friends, my husband's, my children's, my own, and endless arrangements to get together; letters, invitations, telephone calls and transportation hither and yon. . . .

My mind reels with it. What a circus act we women perform every day of our lives. . . .

This is not the life of simplicity but the life of multiplicity that the wise men warn us of. It leads not to unification but to fragmentation. It does not bring grace; it destroys the soul. . . .

96

The problem of the multiplicity of life not only confronts the American woman, but also the American man. And it is not merely the concern of the American as such, but of our whole modern civilization. . . .

Anne Morrow Lindbergh
*Gift from the Sea*

### *Responding* to the Word

You who said, "Come unto me all ye who are weary and heavy-laden and I will give you rest," I come to you now.

For I am weary indeed. Mentally and physically I am bone-tired. I am all wound up, locked up tight with tension. I am too tired to eat. Too tired to think. Too tired even to sleep. I feel close to the point of exhaustion.

Lord, let your healing love flow through me.

I can feel it easing my tensions. Thank you. I can feel my body relaxing. Thank you. I can feel my mind begin to get calm and quiet and composed.

Thank you for unwinding me, Lord, for unlocking me. I am no longer tight and frozen with tiredness, but flowing freely, softly, gently into your healing rest.

Marjorie Holmes
*I've Got to Talk to Somebody, God*

## *Reading* the Word

At that time the disciples came to Jesus, saying, "Who then is greatest in the kingdom of heaven?" And He called a child to Himself and set him before them, and said, "Truly I say to you, unless you are converted and become like children, you shall not enter the kingdom of heaven. Whoever then humbles himself as this child, he is the greatest in the kingdom of heaven." *(Matthew 18:1-4)*

## *Reflecting* on the Word

98

A child has not made up his mind yet about what is and what is not possible. He has no fixed preconceptions about what reality is; and if someone tells him that the mossy place under the lilac bush is a magic place, he may wait until he thinks that no one is watching him, but then he will very probably crawl in under the lilac bush to see for himself. A child also knows how to accept a gift. He does not worry about losing his dignity or becoming indebted if he accepts it. His conscience does not bother him because the gift is free and he has not earned it and therefore really has no right to it. He just takes it, with joy. In fact, if it is something that he wants very much he may even ask for it. And lastly, a child knows how to trust. It is late at night and very dark and there is the sound of sirens as his father wakes him. He does not explain anything but just takes him by the hand and gets him up, and the child is scared out of his wits and has no idea what is going on, but he takes his father's hand anyway and lets his father lead him wherever he chooses into the darkness.

Frederick Buechner
*The Magnificent Defeat*

### *Responding* to the Word

Lord, make me childlike. Deliver me from the urge to compete with another for place or prestige or position. I would be simple and artless as a little child. Deliver me from pose and pretense. Forgive me for thinking of myself. Help me to forget myself and find my true peace in beholding Thee. That Thou mayest answer this prayer, I humble myself before Thee. Lay upon me Thy easy yoke of self-forgetfulness that through it I may find rest. Amen.

A.W. Tozer
*The Pursuit of God*

### *Reading* the Word

Then Peter came and said to Him, "Lord, how often shall my brother sin against me and I forgive him? Up to seven times? Jesus said to him, "I do not say to you, up to seven times, but up to seventy times seven." *(Matthew 18:21-22)*

### *Reflecting* on the Word

To forgive for the moment is not difficult. But to go on forgiving, to forgive the same offense again everytime it recurs to the memory—there's the real tussle.

C.S. Lewis
*Letters to Malcolm*

### *Responding* to the Word

Lord,

How often do I forgive?

I'm asking not for an answer, only for an opportunity
    to come clean.

How often do I forgive?

"Search me, O God, and know my heart."

How often do I forgive the gossiper in my life?

How often do I forgive the exaggerator? The out-and-out liar?

How often do I forgive the talker in my life? The interrupter?

The person who sits around like a bump on a log and says nothing?

How often do I forgive a boss who's demeaning?
A coworker who's competing for my job?
How often do I forgive my mother, for all she did or didn't do?
My father, for all he said or didn't say? My brother? My sister?
"Try me and know my anxious thoughts."
How long is my mental list of hurt feelings?
How far back does the account of "wrongs suffered" go?
"And see if there be any hurtful way in me."
How many people do I mumble to myself about, mentally
    rehearsing the scene where I tell them off and expose them
    to the world?
How many times do I hear bad news about someone who's
    hurt me, and I'm glad because, after all, they had it coming?
"And lead me in the everlasting way."

101

Forgive me, O God, for all the times I haven't forgiven. For all the times I've only partway forgiven, or grudgingly forgiven, or self-righteously forgiven. Lead me into a better way of living, which can only be found in a better way of forgiving. Help me to forgive others the way you have forgiven me.

Not for a moment but for a lifetime.

Not seven times . . . *every* time.

Ken Gire

### *Reading* the Word

Then the righteous will answer Him, saying, "Lord, when did we see You hungry, and feed You, or thirsty, and give You drink? And when did we see You a stranger, and invite You in, or naked, and clothe You? And when did we see You sick, or in prison, and come to You?"

And the King will answer and say to them, "Truly I say to you, to the extent that you did it to one of these brothers of Mine, even to the least of them, you did it to Me."
(*Matthew 25:37-40*)

102

### *Reflecting* on the Word

One of the ways Christ said He speaks to us is through those who are hungry and thirsty, through those who are strangers and those who need clothes, through those who are sick and in prison. And what does He say to us through them?

"Please give me something to eat."

"I'm so thirsty."

"I'm so very lonely. Please stay a while and talk with me."

"Please don't stare. I'm embarrassed enough as it is."

"Please don't be afraid of me. I'm sick, that's all. And I need help."

"I am isolated from everyone in this prison. Please come and visit me."

Just as there are needy people on the street, there are needy people at the office . . . at the factory . . . in the classroom . . . and at home.

"I am hungry," they are saying, and maybe what they are hungry for is just a crust of human kindness.

"I am thirsty," they are saying, and maybe what they are thirsty for is someone who will refresh them with a smile or a pat on the back or an e-mail of encouragement.

"I am lonely," they are saying, and maybe what they are lonely for is someone who will befriend them, understand them, have lunch with them, and listen to them.

Behind all of those voices of hunger and thirst, of loneliness and nakedness, of sickness and imprisonment, behind all of those voices is His voice calling us out of ourselves to Himself.

Ken Gire

103

### *Responding* to the Word

Dear Jesus,

Help me to realize the many voices of hunger, the many sounds of thirst, the many cries of loneliness, the many callings of sickness and nakedness and imprisonment.

Help me to hear in all of them something of you calling to me to become more than I am. More understanding. More compassionate. More involved. More like you.

Ken Gire

## *Reading* the Word

And He asked his father, "How long has this been happening to him?" And he said, "From childhood. And it has often thrown him both into the fire and into the water to destroy him. But if You can do anything, take pity on us and help us!" And Jesus said to him, "If You can! All things are possible to him who believes." Immediately the boy's father cried out and began saying, "I do believe; help my unbelief." *(Mark 9:21-24)*

## *Reflecting* on the Word

104

Faith is a way of looking at what is seen and understanding it in a new sense. Faith is a way of looking at what there is to be seen in the world and in ourselves and hoping, trusting, believing against all evidence to the contrary that beneath the surface we see there is vastly more that we cannot see. . . .

Faith is the eye of the heart, and by faith we see deep down beneath the face of things—by faith we struggle against all odds to be able to see—that the world is God's creation even so. It is he who made us and not we ourselves, made us out of his peace to live in peace, out of his light to dwell in light, out of his love to be above all things loved and loving. That is the last truth about the world.

Can it be true? No of course it cannot. On the face of it, if you take the face seriously and face up to it, how can it possibly be true? Yet how can it not be true when our own hearts bear such powerful witness to it, when blessed moments out of our own lives speak of it so eloquently? And that no-man's-land between the Yes and the No, that everyman's land, is where faith stands and has always stood. Seeing but not seeing, understanding but not understanding, we all stand somewhere between the Yes and the No. . . .

Frederick Buechner

*A Room Called Remember*

### *Responding* to the Word

Lord, I want to love you, yet I'm not sure.
I want to trust you, yet I'm afraid of being taken in.
I know I need you, yet I'm ashamed of the need.
I want to pray, yet I'm afraid of being a hypocrite.
I need my independence, yet I fear to be alone.
I want to belong, yet I must be myself.
Take me, Lord, yet leave me alone.
Lord, I believe; help thou my unbelief.
O Lord, if you are there, you do understand, don't you?
Give me what I need but leave me free to choose.
Help me work it out my own way, but don't let me go.
Let me understand myself, but don't let me despair.
Come unto me, O Lord—I want you there. . . .
Help me to see what I need to do and give me strength to do it.

Bernard, S. S. F.

*The Oxford Book of Prayer*

edited by George Appleton

### *Reading* the Word

And when the sixth hour had come, darkness fell over the whole land until the ninth hour. And at the ninth hour Jesus cried out with a loud voice, "Eloi, Eloi, Lama Sabachthani?" which is translated, "My God, My God, why hast Thou forsaken Me?" *(Mark 15:33-34)*

### *Reflecting* on the Word

It is only one totally blind who puts himself completely into the hands of God, to be led like a child. So to raise the service of the Christian above the human level, the Lord is obliged to plunge him into darkness.

Michel Quoist
*Prayers*

### *Responding* to the Word

My God,
Everything is dark, and you are silent.
For all I know you're on the other side of the world,
going about the business of running a universe.
I don't blame you if you are.
Surely there are more important places for you to be than my
    little corner of the world.

But here,

now,

in my little corner,

it's dark.

Please, don't leave me in the dark.

Don't leave me in silence.

Don't leave me with the hollow sound of my own
  unanswered questions.

I feel like a child, crying out in the middle of the night.

  I am so scared.

Do you know how scared?

Do you care?

Do you even hear me crying?

Why have you forsaken me?

Why here, at such a critical juncture in my life?

Why now, at my age?

My God, my God, why?

Ken Gire

## *Reading* the Word

And the angel said to her, "Do not be afraid, Mary; for you have found favor with God. And behold, you will conceive in your womb, and bear a son, and you shall name Him Jesus. He will be great, and will be called the Son of the Most High." . . . And Mary said, "Behold, the bondslave of the Lord; be it done to me according to your word." *(Luke 1:30-32, 38)*

## *Reflecting* on the Word

108    When God wants an important thing done in this world or a wrong righted, He goes about it in a very singular way. He doesn't release thunderbolts or stir up earthquakes. God simply has a tiny baby born, perhaps of a very humble home, perhaps of a very humble mother. And God puts the idea or purpose into the mother's heart. And she puts it in the baby's mind, and then—God waits. The great events of this world are not battles and elections and earthquakes and thunderbolts. The great events are babies, for each child comes with the message that God is not yet discouraged with humanity, but is still expecting goodwill to become incarnate in each human life.

Edmond McDonald
*Presbyterian Outlook*

### *Responding* to the Word

Dear Lord,

Thank you for how you are fashioning my baby's joints, shaping her face, smoothing her skin. I marvel at the way you work, so patient in your artistry, so painstaking in your attention to detail. Swaddled within the folds of my womb lies a baby I haven't seen or heard or touched, yet I long to know her. In my longing, help me to realize that you long for her too; that you are the one who knew her first, and loved her first; that she was conceived in your mind before she was ever conceived in my body; that she was set apart not to fulfill my will but yours.

Help her to grow pliable to that will, Lord, responsive to every touch of your hand upon her life. Shape within her a spirit so sensitive to spiritual things that she will be able to feel your breath when you whisper to her conscience, sense your shadow when you move across the circumstances of her life.

Use this little girl to mold me, Lord. Use her clinging fingers to make me more gentle and her sudden smile to make me more joyful. Use her countless spills to make me more patient and her helpless cries to make me more compassionate. Use her to mold me not only into more of a mother but more of a human being. . . .

Mary C. Wells and Judy Gire

Robert G. Wells, M.D., and Ken Gire

*Miracle of Life*

109

### *Reading* the Word

And while they were there, the time came for her baby to be born; and she gave birth to her first child, a son. She wrapped him in a blanket and laid him in a manger, because there was no room for them in the village inn. *(Luke 2:6-7, TLB)*

### *Reflecting* on the Word

The child born in the night among beasts. The sweet breath and steaming dung of beasts. And nothing is ever the same again.

110      Those who believe in God can never in a way be sure of him again. Once they have seen him in a stable, they can never be sure where he will appear or to what lengths he will go or to what ludicrous depths of self-humiliation he will descend in his wild pursuit of man. If holiness and the awful power and majesty of God were present in this least auspicious of all events, this birth of a peasant's child, then there is no place or time so lowly and earthbound but that holiness can be present there too. And this means that we are never safe, that there is no place where we can hide from God, no place where we are safe from his power to break in two and recreate the human heart because it is just where he seems most helpless that he is most strong, and just where we least expect him that he comes most fully.

Frederick Buechner
*The Hungering Dark*

### *Responding* to the Word

Holy Child, whom the shepherds and the kings and the dumb beasts adored, be born again. Wherever there is boredom, wherever there is fear of failure, wherever there is temptation too strong to resist, wherever there is bitterness of heart, come, thou blessed one, with healing in thy wings.

Saviour, be born in each of us who raises a face to thy face, not knowing fully who he is or who thou art, knowing only that thy love is beyond his knowing and that no other has the power to make him whole. Come, Lord Jesus, to each who longs for thee even though he has forgotten thy name. Come quickly. Amen.

Frederick Buechner
*The Hungering Dark*

## *Reading* the Word

One of the Pharisees asked Jesus to come to his home for lunch and Jesus accepted the invitation. As they sat down to eat, a woman of the streets—a prostitute—heard he was there and brought an exquisite flask filled with expensive perfume. Going in, she knelt behind him at his feet, weeping, with her tears falling down upon his feet. *(Luke 7:36-38, TLB)*

## *Reflecting* on the Word

You never know what may cause them. The sight of the Atlantic Ocean can do it, or a piece of music, or a face you've never seen before. A pair of somebody's old shoes can do it. Almost any movie made before the great sadness that came over the world after the Second World War, a horse cantering across a meadow, the high school basketball team running out onto the gym floor at the start of a game. You can never be sure. But of this you can be sure. Whenever you find tears in your eyes, especially unexpected tears, it is well to pay the closest attention.

They are not only telling you something about the secret of who you are, but more often than not God is speaking to you through them of the mystery of where you have come from and is summoning you to where, if your soul is to be saved, you should go next.

Frederick Buechner
*Whistling in the Dark*

### *Responding* to the Word

Help me, O God,
Give me the courage to cry.
Help me to understand that tears bring
freshly washed colors arching across the soul,
colors that wouldn't be there apart from the rain.
Help me to see in the prism of my tears,
something of the secret of who I am.
Give me the courage
not only to see what those tears are revealing
but to follow where they are leading.
And help me to see,
somewhere over the rainbow,
that where they are leading me is home. . . .

Ken Gire
*Windows of the Soul*

113

### *Reading* the Word

And a woman who had a hemorrhage for twelve years. . . touched the fringe of His cloak; and immediately her hemorrhage stopped. And Jesus said, "Who is the one who touched Me?" And while they were all denying it, Peter said, "Master, the multitudes are crowding and pressing upon You." But Jesus said, "Someone did touch Me, for I was aware that power had gone out of Me." And when the woman saw that she had not escaped notice, she came trembling and fell down before Him. . . . And He said to her, "Daughter, your faith has made you well; go in peace." *(Luke 8:43-48)*

### *Reflecting* on the Word

*The human touch has the power to arrest God.*
Yes, to stop Him
to halt Him
to make Him aware of your problems,
your pain,
your petition.

"Oh," you say, "that's impossible. God is not interested in me. What does He care what happens to me—one tiny individual in all this creation? Who am I—or what am I that God should take special notice of me?"

Well, there is the record.

There you have it in black and white
that, stopped by the touch of a sick woman, He turned about—
He who conquered death
He who defeated Satan
He whom all the legions of hell cannot stop
He who is King of kings.

He stopped just because a sick and nameless woman touched the hem of His garment.

Peter Marshall
*The Best of Peter Marshall*

115

### *Responding* to the Word

Dear Most Merciful of Physicians,
Help me to realize that it was not the healthy who reached out to you. They bunched up in crowds, but it was those who suffered greatly who reached out to grasp you. . . .

Help me to understand, Lord Jesus, that the hemorrhaging woman's faith was forged on the anvil of twelve long years of suffering. Years of disillusionment. Years of shattered dreams.

Thank you, Lord Jesus, for seeing every hemorrhage in my life through merciful eyes, eyes that understand, eyes that see the whole story of my life. Thank you for your willingness to staunch my suffering. And thank you that I can lay my troubles at your feet and go my way in peace. . . .

Ken Gire
*Intimate Moments with the Savior*

### *Reading* the Word

But wishing to justify himself, he said to Jesus, "And who is my neighbor?"

Jesus replied and said, "A certain man was going down from Jerusalem to Jericho; and he fell among robbers, and they stripped him and beat him, and went off leaving him half dead. And by chance a certain priest was going down on that road, and when he saw him, he passed by on the other side. And likewise a Levite also, when he came to the place and saw him, passed by on the other side. But a certain Samaritan, who was on the journey, came upon him; and when he saw him, he felt compassion, and came to him, and bandaged up his wounds, pouring oil and wine on them; and he put him on his own beast, and brought him to an inn, and took care of him. And on the next day he took out two denarii and gave them to the innkeeper and said, 'Take care of him; and whatever more you spend, when I return, I will repay you.'

"Which of these three do you think proved to be a neighbor to the man who fell into the robbers' hands?" And he said, "The one who showed mercy toward him." And Jesus said to him, "Go and do the same." *(Luke 10:29-37)*

### *Reflecting* on the Word

At any given time, life may cast us in the role of the Good Samaritan or in the role of the man who fell among thieves. Both neighbors are necessary. The play can't go on without them.

Without the Samaritan,

the man who fell among thieves would have died.

Without the man falling among robbers,

something in the Samaritan would have died, too.

The goodness

that was never exercised.

The compassion

that was never spilled.

The sacrifices

that were never made.

The one death may have taken only a few minutes.

The other, a lifetime.

But the absence of either diminishes the other.

Ken Gire

### *Responding* to the Word

I am hungry for neighbors, Lord, true neighbors on whom I can depend and who can depend on me. I long for their occasional companionship, for their understanding, for the knowledge that they are there, willing and wanting to share joy and sorrow with me.

Dear Lord, help me to know who are truly my neighbors, and bring us together so that we can help each other in the timeless ways that neighbors always have.

Marjorie Holmes
*I've Got to Talk to Somebody, God*

## *Reading* the Word

Now as they were traveling along, He entered a certain village; and a woman named Martha welcomed Him into her home. And she had a sister called Mary, who moreover was listening to the Lord's word, seated at His feet. But Martha was distracted with all her preparations; and she came up to Him, and said, "Lord, do You not care that my sister has left me to do all the serving alone? Then tell her to help me." But the Lord answered and said to her, "Martha, Martha, you are worried and bothered about so many things; but only a few things are necessary, really only one, for Mary has chosen the good part, which shall not be taken away from her." *(Luke 10:38-42)*

## *Reflecting* on the Word

Over the years the greatest continuing struggle in the Christian life is the effort to make adequate time for daily waiting on God, weekly inventory, and monthly planning. Since this time for receiving marching orders is so important, Satan will do everything he can to squeeze it out. Yet we know from experience that only by this means can we escape the tyranny of the urgent.

This is how Jesus succeeded. He did not finish all the urgent tasks in Palestine or all the things he may have liked to do, but he did finish the work which God gave him to do.

The only alternative to frustration is to be sure that we

are doing what God wants. Nothing substitutes for knowing that this day, this hour, in this place we are doing the will of the Father.

Charles E. Hummel
*Tyranny of the Urgent*

### *Responding* to the Word

Father, I need Thee to teach me day by day, according to each day's opportunities and needs. My ears are dull, so that I cannot hear Thy voice; my eyes are dim, so that I cannot see Thy tokens. Thou alone canst quicken my hearing, and purge my sight, and cleanse and renew my heart. Teach me to sit at Thy feet, and to hear Thy voice. Amen.

119

John Henry Newman
quoted in *My Favorite Prayers*
by Norman Vincent Peale

### *Reading* the Word

And it came about that while He was praying in a certain place, after He had finished, one of His disciples said to Him, "Lord, teach us to pray just as John also taught his disciples." And He said to them, "When you pray, say:

'Father, hallowed be Thy name.

Thy kingdom come.

Give us each day our daily bread.

And forgive us our sins,

For we ourselves also forgive everyone who is indebted to us.

And lead us not into temptation.'"

And He said to them, "Suppose one of you shall have a friend, and shall go to him at midnight, and say to him, 'Friend, lend me three loaves; for a friend of mine has come to me from a journey, and I have nothing to set before him'; and from inside he shall answer and say, 'Do not bother me; the door has already been shut and my children and I are in bed; I cannot get up and give you anything.'

"I tell you, even though he will not get up and give him anything because he is his friend, yet because of his persistence he will get up and give him as much as he needs. And I say to you, ask, and it shall be given to you; seek, and you shall find; knock, and it shall be opened to you. For everyone who asks receives; and he who seeks finds; and to him who knocks it shall be opened. Now suppose one of you fathers is asked by his son for a fish; he will not give him a snake instead of a fish, will he? Or if he is asked for an egg, he will not give him a scorpion, will he? If you then, being evil, know how to give good gifts to your children, how much more shall your Heavenly Father give the Holy Spirit to those who ask Him?" *(Luke 11:1-13)*

### *Reflecting* on the Word

It is significant to note that though Jesus never taught his disciples how to preach, he did teach them how to pray.

Ray Stedman
*Jesus Teaches on Prayer*

121

### *Responding* to the Word

Lord,
Teach me to pray. Teach me to come to you with the outstretched arms of a child who runs to its father for comfort. As I come, fill me with all the love, all the respect, all the honor that a child should have for a parent.

Take my small clumsy hands in yours and walk with me, Lord. Lead the way through the dark streets. And help me to keep pace with you so that your will would be done in my life here on earth as it is in heaven. . . .

Ken Gire
*Instructive Moments with the Savior*

## *Reading* the Word

And someone in the crowd said to Him, "Teacher, tell my brother to divide the family inheritance with me." But He said to him, "Man, who appointed Me a judge and arbiter over you?" And He said to them, "Beware, and be on your guard against every form of greed; for not even when one has an abundance does his life consist of possessions." And He told them a parable, saying, "The land of a certain rich man was very productive. And he began reasoning to himself, saying, 'What shall I do, since I have no place to store my crops?' And he said, 'This is what I will do: I will tear down my barns and build larger ones, and there I will store all my grain and my goods. And I will say to my soul, "Soul, you have many goods laid up for many years to come; take your ease, eat, drink and be merry." ' But God said to him, 'You fool! This very night your soul is required of you; and now who will own what you have?' So is the man who lays up treasure for himself, and is not rich toward God." *(Luke 12:13-21)*

## *Reflecting* on the Word

A man must keep things at their distance. He must be *in* the material world, but not *of* it. He must say to his possessions: "You are not my life. You never can be my life. There is a gulf set between you and me." The gulf is proved because his possessions cannot even answer him! But the Rich Man thought so persistently and with such concentration about his "goods" that the necessary line of distinction between *him* and *his* was erased. His life was lost in his livelihood. . . . He had no thought for God. "*My* fruits," he called them; "*my* grain." But in what sense were they his? Could he command the sap in the tree, the fertility in the soil? Were sunrise and sunset under his control? Was the Faithfulness of returning seasons his merit? If the rain had been withheld, where then would have been his wealth: "The *ground* brought forth plentifully"; all the man could do was to take nature's tides at the flood. He was carried to fortune on a fecundity, a light, a heat, a constancy in nature's cycles, which are boundless mysteries of blessing—and he called them "mine"! His title was earned—"Thou fool!"

123

George Buttrick
*The Parables of Jesus*

### *Responding* to the Word

Dear God,

I so much want to be in control.

I want to be the master of my own destiny.

Still I know you are saying:

"Let me take you by the hand and lead you. Accept my love and trust that where I will bring you, the deepest desires of your heart will be fulfilled."

Lord, open my hands to receive your gift of love. Amen.

Henri Nouwen
*With Open Hands*

### *Reading* the Word

Therefore He was saying, "What is the kingdom of God like, and to what shall I compare it? It is like a mustard seed, which a man took and threw into his own garden; and it grew and became a tree; and the birds of the air nested in its branches." *(Luke 13:18-19)*

### *Reflecting* on the Word

If you will cling to Nature, to the simple in Nature, to the little things that hardly anyone sees, and that can so unexpectedly become big and beyond measuring; if you have this love of inconsiderable things and seek quite simply, as one who serves, to win the confidence of what seems poor: then everything will become easier, more coherent and somehow more conciliatory for you. . . .

Rainer Maria Rilke
*Letters to a Young Poet*

### *Responding* to the Word

Lord of little things
you made your home
in a stable under a star
in a cradle on straw
and the little things
shone their starlit welcome

make your home with me
in the little things of my days
cards, gifts, mistletoe on tiptoe
tree tinsel, multicolored lights
and let the little things
shine their glory for you and me
once more. . . .

Robert A. Raines
*Living the Questions*

### *Reading* the Word

Whoever does not carry his own cross and come after Me cannot be My disciple. *(Luke 14:27)*

### *Reflecting* on the Word

The cross is laid on every Christian. The first Christ-suffering which every man must experience is the call to abandon the attachments of this world. It is that dying of the old man which is the result of his encounter with Christ. As we embark upon discipleship we surrender ourselves to Christ in union with his death—we give over our lives to death. Thus it begins; the cross is not the terrible end to an otherwise god-fearing and happy life, but it meets us at the beginning of our communion with Christ. When Christ calls a man, he bids him come and die. It may be a death like that of the first disciples who had to leave home and work to follow him, or it may be a death like Luther's, who had to leave the monastery and go out into the world. But it is the same death every time—death in Jesus Christ, the death of the old man at his call.

Dietrich Bonhoeffer
*The Cost of Discipleship*

### *Responding* to the Word

Dearest Lord, teach me to be generous.
Teach me to serve you as you deserve;
To give and not to count the cost;
To fight and not to heed the wounds;
To toil and not to seek for rest;
To labor and not seek reward,
Save that of knowing that I do your will.

St. Ignatius of Loyola

## *Reading* the Word

And a certain ruler questioned Him, saying, "Good Teacher, what shall I do to obtain eternal life?" And Jesus said to him, "Why do you call Me good? No one is good except God alone. You know the commandments, 'Do not commit adultery, do not murder, do not steal, do not bear false witness, honor your father and mother.'" And he said, "All these things I have kept from my youth." And when Jesus heard this, He said to him, "One thing you still lack; sell all that you possess, and distribute it to the poor, and you shall have treasure in heaven; and come, follow Me." But when he had heard these things, he became very sad; for he was extremely rich. And Jesus looked at him and said, "How hard it is for those who are wealthy to enter the kingdom of God! For it is easier for a camel to go through the eye of a needle, than for a rich man to enter the kingdom of God." *(Luke 18:18-25)*

## *Reflecting* on the Word

The value of money, like stocks and bonds, goes up and down for reasons not even the experts can explain and at moments nobody can predict, so you can be a millionaire one moment and a pauper the next without lifting a finger. Great fortunes can be made and lost completely on paper. There is more concrete reality in a baby's throwing its rattle out of the crib.

There are people who use up their entire lives making

money so they can enjoy the lives they have entirely used up.

Jesus says that it's easier for a camel to go through the eye of a needle than for a rich man to enter the Kingdom of God. Maybe the reason is not that the rich are so wicked they're kept out of the place but that they're so out of touch with reality they can't see it's a place worth getting into.

Frederick Buechner
*Whistling in the Dark*

### *Responding* to the Word

Lord, help me to remember how generously you have endowed the earth.

That you have lavished upon us more food than any of us can consume. More clothing than any of us can wear. More treasures than we can carry.

And that it is your will that each of us have his portion. A fine full portion to meet all our needs.

Help me to realize what my real needs are. And to be thankful. For so long as I trust in you all those needs are being, and will be met. . . .

(You said it is hard for a rich man to enter the kingdom of heaven. Perhaps it's even harder for a poor man who wants to be rich!)

Marjorie Holmes
*I've Got to Talk to Somebody, God*

### *Reading* the Word

And when He approached, He saw the city and wept over it, saying, "If you had known in this day, even you, the things which make for peace! But now they have been hidden from your eyes. For the days shall come upon you when your enemy will throw up a bank before you, and surround you, and hem you in on every side, and will level you to the ground and your children within you, and they will not leave in you one stone upon another, because you did not recognize the time of your visitation."
*(Luke 19:41-44)*

130

### *Reflecting* on the Word

When Jesus preached repentance, when Jesus wept over Jerusalem, which even then would not recognize the things that make for peace, he did so in a voice almost choked with tears. How is it that the language of the Bible, which is normally so strong and unsentimental, should at this point speak of tears? Jesus wept not only because these were his people who were lurching so unavertibly toward the abyss. No, Jesus wept because he knew the power of the Seducer, the menacing mystery of the devil, who seizes even the upright, the respectable, the morally intact people by the throat, and grips them in such a way that at first even they themselves (if they do not have the gift of distinguishing between spirits) have no premonition of the dreadful slopes to which they are being edged by a consummate cunning.

Helmut Thielicke

*Life Can Begin Again*

### *Responding* to the Word

Lord Jesus,

Help me to understand the weight you carried on that long road to Jerusalem. How much destruction did you see beyond the rubble of the temple? How many nations did you see beating their plows into swords and their pruning hooks into spears? How many Stalins and Hitlers did you see gathering darkly on the political horizon?

131

How many genocides did you witness because there was no peace between nations? How many homicides, because there was no peace between neighbors? How many suicides, because there was no peace in the human heart?

How much racial hatred did you see with those tear-filled eyes? How much fighting under the banner of religion? How much injustice?

How much, Lord, did you see? How much did you feel? How many tears did those eyes of yours cry ? . . .

Ken Gire

*Moments with the Savior*

### *Reading* the Word

And He came out and proceeded as was His custom to the Mount of Olives; and the disciples also followed Him. And when He arrived at the place, He said to them, "Pray that you may not enter into temptation." And He withdrew from them about a stone's throw, and He knelt down and began to pray, saying, "Father, if Thou art willing, remove this cup from Me; yet not My will, but Thine be done." *(Luke 22:39-42)*

### *Reflecting* on the Word

132

Imagine life to be like a woven rug. Science sees the patterned threads from the earthbound side of the frame, not in their weaving but only when they have been woven, and traces their regularities. Great art in music and drama stands likewise, and glories in the color and imagination of the design. But prayer stands with the Weaver as He works. The Weaver says in graciousness: "You shall help me in prayer and thought and labor, though for your own good I still must guide. Some of your wishes shall be granted, for through the granting you shall more surely learn: and I will still guide. Some of your wishes cannot be granted. When the design is complete, and you can see it from the other side of time, you will understand. And your best prayer is still the prayer of Christ, 'Not my will, but. . . . '"

George Buttrick

*Prayer*

## *Responding* to the Word

Today, O Lord, I yield myself to you.
May your will be my delight today.
May your way have perfect sway in me.
May your love be the pattern of my living.

I surrender to you my hopes,
my dreams,
my ambitions.
Do with them what you will, when you will, as you will.

I place into your loving care
my family,
my friends,
my future.
Care for them with a care that I can never give.

133

I release into your hands
my need to control,
my craving for status,
my fear of obscurity. . . .

For Jesus' sake, Amen.

Richard Foster
*Prayers from the Heart*

### *Reading* the Word

And behold, two of them were going that very day to a village named Emmaus. . . . And it came about that while they were conversing and discussing, Jesus Himself approached, and began traveling with them. But their eyes were prevented from recognizing Him. And He said to them, "What are these words that you are exchanging with one another as you are walking?" And they stood still, looking sad. And one of them, named Cleopas, answered and said to Him, "Are You the only one visiting Jerusalem and unaware of the things which have happened here in these days?" And He said to them, "What things?" And they said to Him, "The things about Jesus the Nazarene, who was a prophet mighty in deed and word in the sight of God and all the people, and how the chief priests and our rulers delivered Him up to the sentence of death, and crucified Him. But we were hoping that it was He who was going to redeem Israel. Indeed, besides all this, it is the third day since these things happened." *(Luke 24:13-21)*

134

### *Reflecting* on the Word

Emmaus is whatever we do or wherever we go to make ourselves forget that the world holds nothing sacred: that even the wisest and bravest and loveliest decay and die; that even the noblest ideas that men have had—ideas about love and freedom and justice—have always in time been twisted out of shape by selfish men for selfish ends. Emmaus is where we go, where these two went, to try to forget about Jesus and the great failure of his life. . . .

It is precisely at such times as these that life is going to ask questions about where the road we are traveling is finally going to take us; about whether food is enough to keep us alive, truly alive; about who we are and who the stranger is behind us.

In other words, it is precisely as such times as these that Jesus is apt to come, into the very midst of life at its most real and inescapable.

Frederick Buechner      135
*The Magnificent Defeat*

### *Responding* to the Word

Lord, it's good to know you are with me,
in all the strains life brings.
In the disappointments and difficulties
let me feel your presence.
And, Lord, help me share this with others.
Make my presence with them your presence.
May your Spirit in me encourage and strengthen.
And as I recognise Jesus walking beside me,
may others see something of him in me. . . .

Eddie Askew
*A Silence and a Shouting*

### *Reading* the Word

The Word became flesh and blood, and moved into the neighborhood. *(John 1:14, TM)*

### *Reflecting* on the Word

Not passed through. Not visited. Moved into.

It would be like the President of the United States moving into south central Los Angeles. Not passing through in a motorcade. Not visiting for a photo opportunity. Moving in. Think of it. The President. Moving out of the White House and into some housing project. The President, moving out of the Oval Office and away from Pennsylvania Avenue, sharing not only our street address but our living conditions. Living among the broken glass and the graffiti. Among the rats and the cockroaches. Among the hookers and the panhandlers. Among the drug dealers and the drive-by shootings.

The President of the United States. Moving into that neighborhood. Leaving behind scores of secret service agents assigned to protect him. Leaving behind a press secretary whose job it was to clarify his message and correct any misperceptions the people might have. Leaving behind all whose responsibility it was to attend to his every wish.

That is what the King of the Universe did when He became flesh and blood. That is what He left behind. That is what He shared. That is what He subjected Himself to.

To the poverty of the street. To the heartache of the street. To the temptations of the street. And its violence. Which, in the end, would find Him. Corner Him in some dark alley. Strip Him of what little possessions He had. And murder Him.

That was the kind of neighborhood it was. And Jesus knew that. Even before He moved in.

Ken Gire

### *Responding* to the Word

See, he's half-hidden by the curtain that's moving a little in the breeze. That tenement—it's a poor place to have to live, isn't it, Jesus?

He is seated alone by a kitchen table and looking blankly out the window. . . . There is nothing for him to do. He doesn't have any money; all he has is time.

Who is he in my life, Jesus? What has he got to do with me? He's your brother, and you love him. What does this say to me, Lord? . . . I mean, how can I possibly be responsible in any honest, meaningful way for that guy?

He just moved a short bit away from the window. Maybe he moved because he felt my eyes on him from the sidewalk down here. I didn't mean to embarrass him, Lord; I just wanted to let him know somebody understands he's alive and he's your brother, so he's not alone or lost. Does he know it, Jesus?

Malcolm Boyd
*Are You Running with Me, Jesus?*

### *Reading* the Word

We all live off his generous bounty, gift after gift after gift.
*(John 1:16, TM)*

### *Reflecting* on the Word

Most of what we have we've worked for, haven't we? By the sweat of our brow and the labor of our hands. But who gave us those hands? And the strength to use them? And the mind to coordinate them? Were they not all gifts?

138

Or maybe our work is mental not manual, and we are where we are in life because of years of education. But who gave us the mind to utilize that education? Who integrated the circuitry for the storage and retrieval of our thoughts? Who provided the neurological current that even makes our thoughts possible?

Or maybe our work revolves around certain issues burning in our heart, and that's why we're a social worker or a judge or why we volunteer at a homeless shelter. We live and work by the dictates of our conscience. But who did the dictation? Truth, justice, a sense of right and wrong, compassion.

Where did these grand notions originate? With us? Were they not engraved on our heart the way the commandments were etched on stone? Were they not also gifts? The love we give. The love given to us. Was it not a gift? And faith, that most primal of spiritual responses, did it not also come to us as a gift?

The air we breathe. A gift. The lungs to breathe it. A gift.

The involuntary muscles that keep us breathing. A gift. Our waking to a new day. A gift.

Whatever we start with, if we follow it far enough back, the source is God and His generosity in sharing it. It's all a gift. Everything. We live, quite literally, off His generous bounty.

So great the generosity. So little the gratitude. Yet still He gives. Gift after gift after gift.

Ken Gire

### *Responding* to the Word

Oh God, you who brought me, without consulting me, without my knowledge of what you were doing or why, into this difficult and puzzling but also fascinating world, help me to trust you to know what you're doing.

I owe every single thing I have, and am, and know, and enjoy, and love, to your generosity, initiative, intelligence, and power . . . all summed up in the all-encompassing phrase "creative love." . . .

Teach me to be trusting, instead of cynical; peaceful, instead of quarrelsome; humble, instead of arrogant. Teach me to stop thinking I know more and better than the Being that gave me my being!

Joan Bel Geddes
*Are You Listening God?*

### *Reading* the Word

Jesus said to her, "Woman, believe Me, an hour is coming when neither in this mountain, nor in Jerusalem, shall you worship the Father. You worship that which you do not know; we worship that which we know, for salvation is from the Jews. But an hour is coming, and now is, when the true worshipers shall worship the Father in spirit and truth; for such people the Father seeks to be His worshipers." *(John 4:21-23)*

### *Reflecting* on the Word

140

Everything the church is supposed to do in this world is a by-product of spiritual worship, and that includes evangelism, missions, giving, works of mercy, education, and personal holiness and service. First God calls us to worship, then He sends us out to witness and to work. God wants worship to come first, for only then will we be energized by His power and bring glory to His name. Worship puts God where He deserves to be and keeps man where he ought to be.

Warren W. Wiersbe
*The Integrity Crisis*

### *Responding* to the Word

Eternal Father of my soul, let my first thought today be of Thee, let my first impulse be to worship Thee, let my first speech be

Thy name, let my first action be to kneel before Thee in prayer.

For Thy perfect wisdom and perfect goodness:
For the love wherewith Thou lovest mankind:
For the love wherewith Thou lovest me:
For the great and mysterious opportunity of my life:
For the indwelling of Thy Spirit in my heart:
For the sevenfold gifts of Thy Spirit:
I praise and worship Thee, O Lord.

Yet let me not, when this morning prayer is said, think my worship ended and spend the day in forgetfulness of Thee. Rather from these moments of quietness let light go forth, and joy, and power, that will remain with me through all the hours of the day. . . . .

John Baillie
*A Diary of Private Prayer*

141

## *Reading* the Word

I am the bread of life; he who comes to Me shall not hunger. . . .
*(John 6:35)*

## *Reflecting* on the Word

When the bread of heaven came down and offered himself to the public, people came from miles around, lining up, hoping some small crust of something good might fall their way.

But Jesus returned to heaven and for a while there was no bread. In his absence, though, he made sure the world would not go hungry.

He left the recipe for his life in the Scriptures. And he left his Spirit to blend its truths into our lives—flour and sugar, raw eggs and butter, everything. From there, the bare hands of circumstance were called in to knead the dough, a time of solitude was set aside to give the loaf a chance to rise, and the ovens of daily life were opened to bake it.

And once again, the aroma of freshly baked bread filled the earth.

Ken Gire
*Windows of the Soul*

142

### *Responding* to the Word

Help me, O God,

To live the recipe
before I give the recipe.
Give me the kneading strength
to work the words into the doughy recesses of my life.
Help me to leave it alone a while
so it can rise.
Help me not to fear the oven
so it can bake.
And grant that in the baking,
the world would be able to roll down its window
and savor the aroma of freshly baked bread. . . .

Ken Gire
*Windows of the Soul*

143

### *Reading* the Word

They brought to the Pharisees him who was formerly blind. Now it was the Sabbath on the day when Jesus made the clay, and opened his eyes. Again, therefore, the Pharisees also were asking him how he received his sight. And he said to them, "He applied clay to my eyes, and I washed, and I see." Therefore some of the Pharisees were saying, "This man is not from God, because He does not keep the Sabbath." But others were saying, "How can a man who is a sinner perform such signs?" And there was a division among them. . . . He therefore answered, "Whether He is a sinner, I do not know; one thing I do know, that, whereas I was blind, now I see." *(John 9:13-16, 25)*

144

### *Reflecting* on the Word

Agnes Sanford says: "Religion is an experience of God. Theology is merely an attempt to explain the experience."

Well, who needs it (except the theologians)? What most of us really need is the experience. And for me, at least, theology can actually hinder, get between. Theology is like trying to enjoy the rainbow with somebody at your side analyzing it for you. Or it's like thrilling to a poem and then having some teacher tear it apart. Or Robert Frost's "Stopping by the Woods on a Snowy Evening," which John Ciardi took five thousand words to explain . . . and Frost's amusement: "Gee, I didn't know I'd meant all that." Critics and theologians can read all sorts of meanings into things even an author never intended.

So I think it must be with God, who must stand back in amazement sometimes at the tomes of literature written to "explain" religion to the masses. As if we are too dumb to understand our own experience.

Marjorie Holmes
*How Can I Find You, God?*

### *Responding* to the Word

I no longer want just to hear about you, beloved Lord, through messengers. I no longer want to hear doctrines about you, nor to have my emotions stirred by people speaking of you. I yearn for your presence.

These messengers simply frustrate and grieve me, because they remind me of how distant I am from you. They reopen wounds in my heart, and they seem to delay your coming to me.

From this day onwards please send me no more messengers, no more doctrines, because they cannot satisfy my overwhelming desire for you.

I want to give myself completely to you.

And I want you to give yourself completely to me.

The love which you show in glimpses, reveal to me fully. The love which you convey through messengers, speak it to me directly. I sometimes think you are mocking me by hiding yourself from me. Come to me with the priceless jewel of your love.

St. John of the Cross

### *Reading* the Word

Jesus, therefore, six days before the Passover, came to Bethany where Lazarus was, whom Jesus had raised from the dead. So they made Him a supper there, and Martha was serving; but Lazarus was one of those reclining at the table with Him. Mary therefore took a pound of very costly perfume of pure nard, and anointed the feet of Jesus, and wiped His feet with her hair; and the house was filled with the fragrance of the perfume. But Judas Iscariot, one of His disciples, who was intending to betray Him, said, "Why was this perfume not sold for three hundred denarii, and given to poor people?" Now he said this, not because he was concerned about the poor, but because he was a thief, and as he had the money box, he used to pilfer what was put into it. Jesus therefore said, "Let her alone, in order that she may keep it for the day of My burial. For the poor you always have with you, but you do not always have Me." *(John 12:1-8)*

### *Reflecting* on the Word

I spent a lot of time in seminary studying the Bible, and it led me to a lot of places. Hebrew. Greek. Systematic Theology. Hermeneutics. A lot of good places. And at those places I learned a lot of important things. But it was Mary, in an intimate moment with the Savior, who taught me what was most important. And it wasn't how pure my doctrine was. It was how passionate my devotion. That was what mattered to Jesus. . . .

The pictures dear to Jesus, the ones he holds close to his heart, the ones that bring a tear to his eyes or a smile to his face are ones like Mary's. Because what touches his heart is not how much we know, but how much we love.

Ken Gire
*Windows of the Soul*

### *Responding* to the Word

Help me, O God,

To treasure all the words in the Scriptures,                    147
but to treasure them only as they lead to You.
May the words be stepping stones in finding You,
and if I am to get lost at all in the search,
may it not be down a theological rabbit trail,
or in some briar patch of religious controversy.
If I am to get lost at all,
grant that it be in Your arms.
Help me to love You the way Mary did.
And may something of the spilling passion of her devotion,
    spill onto me.

Ken Gire
*Windows of the Soul*

### *Reading* the Word

"Father, glorify Thy name." There came therefore a voice out of heaven: "I have both glorified it, and will glorify it again." The multitude therefore, who stood by and heard it, were saying that it had thundered; others were saying, "An angel has spoken to Him." Jesus answered and said, "This voice has not come for My sake, but for your sakes." *(John 12:28-30)*

### *Reflecting* on the Word

148 When God spoke out of heaven to our Lord, self-centered men who heard it explained it by natural causes, saying, "It thundered." The habit of explaining the Voice by appeals to natural law is at the very root of modern science. In the living, breathing cosmos there is a mysterious Something, too wonderful, too awful for any mind to understand. The believing man does not claim to understand. He falls to his knees and whispers, "God." The man of earth kneels also, but not to worship. He kneels to examine, to search, to find the cause and the how of things. Just now we happen to be living in a secular age. Our thought habits are those of the scientist, not those of the worshipper. We are more likely to explain than to adore. "It thundered," we exclaim, and go our earthly way. But still the Voice sounds and searches.

The order and life of the world depend upon that Voice, but men are mostly too busy or too stubborn to give attention.

A.W. Tozer

*The Pursuit of God*

### *Responding* to the Word

Lord, teach me to listen. The times are noisy and my ears are weary with the thousand raucous sounds which continuously assault them. Give me the spirit of the boy Samuel when he said to Thee, "Speak, for thy servant heareth." Let me hear Thee speaking in my heart. Let me get used to the sound of Thy voice, that its tones may be familiar when the sounds of the earth die away and the only sound will be the music of Thy speaking voice. Amen.

149

A.W. Tozer

*The Pursuit of God*

## *Reading* the Word

Let not your heart be troubled; believe in God, believe also in Me. In My Father's house are many dwelling places; if it were not so, I would have told you; for I go to prepare a place for you. And if I go and prepare a place for you, I will come again, and receive you to Myself; that where I am, there you may be also. *(John 14:1-3)*

## *Reflecting* on the Word

150 The Christian doctrine of suffering explains, I believe, a very curious fact about the world we live in. The settled happiness and security which we all desire, God withholds from us by the very nature of the world: but joy, pleasure, and merriment He has scattered broadcast. We are never safe, but we have plenty of fun, and some ecstasy. It is not hard to see why. The security we crave would teach us to rest our hearts in this world and [pose] an obstacle to our return to God: a few moments of happy love, a landscape, a symphony, a merry meeting with our friends, a [swim] or a football match, have no such tendency. Our Father refreshes us on the journey with some pleasant inns, but will not encourage us to mistake them for home.

C.S. Lewis
*The Problem of Pain*

### *Responding* to the Word

Dear Lord Jesus,

Thank you that here and there you have shown me glimpses of heaven, however briefly. That now and then you have sent me echoes of it, however faintly. And that once in a while you have allowed it to touch me, however gently. Those glimpses, those echoes, those touches have awakened my longing for home, and for each one of those awakenings, I thank you.

Thank you that I have a room in your Father's house. A place just for me. Thank you for all you have done to ready it for my arrival. For all the longings that lead me there and for all the reminders that let me know that this is not my home, I thank you, O Lord. Remind me often, for so often I forget, that the very best of homes here on earth is just a shadow of the home waiting for me in heaven.

Ken Gire

*Moments with the Savior*

151

## *Reading* the Word

Do you not believe that I am in the Father, and the Father is in Me? The words that I say to you I do not speak on My own initiative, but the Father abiding in Me does His works. Believe Me that I am in the Father, and the Father in Me; otherwise believe on account of the works themselves. Truly, truly, I say to you, he who believes in me, the works that I do shall he do also; and greater works than these shall he do; because I go to the Father. *(John 14:10-12)*

152

## *Reflecting* on the Word

God is a kind Father. He sets us all in the places where He wishes us to be employed; and that employment is truly "our Father's business." He chooses work for every creature which will be delightful to them, if they do it simply and humbly. He gives us always strength enough, and sense enough, for what He wants us to do; if we either tire ourselves or puzzle ourselves, it is our own fault. And we may always be sure, whatever we are doing, that we cannot be pleasing Him, if we are not happy ourselves.

J. Ruskin

quoted in *Daily Strength for Daily Needs*

by Mary W. Tileston

### *Responding* to the Word

God, I am scurrying around like a chicken with her head cut off, making a mess everywhere I light.

Why, God, when I know if I wait quietly and listen for Your guidance, I do better and work more efficiently, do I rush about—driven by time, rather than by You?

Help me, God, to slow down, to be silent, so I can hear You and do Your will and not mine.

Marian Wright Edelman
*Guide My Feet*

153

## *Reading* the Word

But the Helper, the Holy Spirit, whom the Father will send in My name, He will teach you all things, and bring to your remembrance all that I said to you. (*John 14:26*)

## *Reflecting* on the Word

The early days of my walk in the Spirit were full of exciting discoveries. After all, the gospel narratives are startlingly brief. There is so much not told us, so many gaps. Mostly, we are given principles as guidelines, but the question always is, how does this work out in everyday life? How do I apply this in my workaday world?

Jesus' words about the Spirit teaching us all things and bringing to our remembrance all that Jesus has said, are one such guideline. My exciting discovery was that Jesus' promise is much more inclusive than we have thought or dreamed. Once started on my walk in the Spirit, I found that the Helper had quietly become the living Repository of my memory and my mind—that incredibly intricate human brain that still baffles all scientists—the Chief Librarian of my lifetime storehouse of memories, thoughts, quotations, all kinds of specific data.

He was now in charge of the whole, and I could trust Him to find and bring up out of the voluminous "stacks" of memory whatever I needed. There were those everyday gaps in memory when I could not recall a person's name or the name of a street or a book or a verse of Scripture. The Spirit was eager to

154

come to my assistance. When I asked Him for this help and then released the problem from my mind, usually not immediately, but within hours, the Helper would deliver the answer.

Catherine Marshall
*The Helper*

### *Responding* to the Word

Lord, I confess that I have been reluctant to admit You into my daily life in relation to small, intimate needs. I had not thought that the Lord of the universe, high and lifted up, should be bothered with my little problems. Yet here You are making it clear to us that the Helper will be as close to us as our own thoughts, supplying even needed information and reminding us in a critical moment of Your words of promise and blessing.

155

Thank you too for putting Your finger so incisively on a deeper reason for my reluctance to admit You to the minutiae of my life. I have been afraid of the fair exchange You are asking of me: the Helper will supply everything—even these small needs—in exchange for my whole life. Not only does He want to use me, He wants an exuberance of giving on both sides.

Lord, melt away any pockets of resistance left. Don't let me hug any part of my life to myself. Show me today how to take at least one definite step of trusting the Helper. Thank You, Lord. Amen.

Catherine Marshall
*The Helper*

### *Reading* the Word

Peace I leave with you; My peace I give to you; not as the world gives, do I give to you. . . . *(John 14:27)*

### *Reflecting* on the Word

God's mark of approval, whenever you obey Him, is peace. He sends an immeasurable, deep peace; not a natural peace, "as the world gives," but the peace of Jesus. Whenever peace does not come, wait until it does, or seek to find out why it is not coming. If you are acting on your own impulse, or out of a sense of the heroic, to be seen by others, the peace of Jesus will not exhibit itself. This shows no unity with God or confidence in Him. The spirit of simplicity, clarity, and unity is born through the Holy Spirit, not through your decisions. God counters our self-willed decisions with an appeal for simplicity and unity.

My questions arise whenever I cease to obey. When I do obey God, problems come, not between me and God, but as a means to keep my mind examining with amazement the revealed truth of God. But any problem that comes between God and myself is the result of disobedience. Any problem that comes while I obey God (and there will be many), increases my overjoyed delight, because I know that my Father knows and cares, and I can watch and anticipate how He will unravel my problems.

Oswald Chambers
*My Utmost for His Highest*

156

### *Responding* to the Word

Show us, good Lord,

The peace we should seek

The peace we must give

The peace we can keep

The peace we must forgo,

And the peace you have given in Jesus our Lord.

Contemporary Prayers for Public Worship

*Life's Little Prayer Book*

compiled by Gary Lahoda

157

## *Reading* the Word

I am the true vine, and My Father is the vinedresser. Every branch in Me that does not bear fruit, He takes away; and every branch that bears fruit, He prunes it, that it may bear more fruit. *(John 15:1-2)*

## *Reflecting* on the Word

In pruning a vine, two principles are generally observed: first, all dead wood must be ruthlessly removed; and second, the live wood must be cut back drastically. Dead wood harbors insects and disease and may cause the vine to rot, to say nothing of being unproductive and unsightly. Live wood must be trimmed back in order to prevent such heavy growth that the life of the vine goes into the wood rather than into fruit. The vineyards in the early spring look like a collection of barren, bleeding stumps; but in the fall they are filled with luxuriant purple grapes. As the farmer wields the pruning knife on his vines, so God cuts dead wood out from among His saints, and often cuts back the living wood so far that His method seems cruel. Nevertheless, from those who have suffered the most there often comes the greatest fruitfulness.

Merrill C. Tenney
*John: The Gospel of Belief*

### *Responding* to the Word

Somehow, in the midst of it, I realized I could not go it alone, Lord. It was too much. I could not handle the weight of it, the people, the problems, the family, my job as a wife and mother, my fate as a woman in this demanding world, without support beyond my own.

Those words in John—all of them—must have been written for me: "Abide in me, and I in you. As the branch cannot bear fruit of itself, except it abide in the vine; no more can ye, except ye abide in me. I am the vine, ye are the branches: He that abideth in me, and I in him, the same bringeth forth much fruit: for without me ye can do nothing" (John 15:4-5).

I was like that. I saw that without you I could do nothing. You are the vine, not me. Weak and faulty as I was, I'd been trying to be the vine, holding up all the branches. I was just a branch and I had to be pruned, I had to be stripped if my roots were to be strengthened. Then only then could I bring forth much fruit!

Marjorie Holmes
*How Can I Find You, God?*

### *Reading* the Word

Abide in Me, and I in you. As the branch cannot bear fruit of itself, unless it abides in the vine, so neither can you, unless you abide in Me. I am the vine, you are the branches; he who abides in Me, and I in him, he bears much fruit; for apart from Me, you can do nothing. *(John 15:4-5)*

### *Reflecting* on the Word

Christ used the illustration of the branch and the vine to show what it meant to remain in Him. The branch has no life in itself; it draws its life from the vine. The branch is nourished and sustained by the life of the vine. As long as there is an uninterrupted flow of life from the vine into the branch, the branch is capable of bearing fruit. The moment the branch is severed from the life of the vine, it is rendered incapable of bearing fruit. What was true in the natural realm was most certainly true of these men in their forthcoming ministry.

J. Dwight Pentecost
*The Words and Works of Jesus Christ*

### *Responding* to the Word

Let us all become a true and fruitful branch on the vine Jesus, by accepting Him in our lives as it pleases Him to come:

as the Truth—to be told;

160

as the Life—to be lived;
as the Light—to be lighted;
as the Love—to be loved;
as the Way—to be walked;
as the Joy—to be given;
as the Peace—to be spread;
as the Sacrifice—to be offered,
in our families and within our neighborhood.

Mother Teresa
*A Simple Path*

### *Reading* the Word

So when they had finished breakfast, Jesus said to Simon Peter, "Simon, son of John, do you love Me more than these?" He said to Him, "Yes, Lord; You know that I love You." He said to him, "Tend My lambs." He said to him again a second time, "Simon, son of John, do you love Me?" He said to Him, "Yes, Lord; You know that I love You." He said to him, "Shepherd My sheep." He said to him the third time, "Simon, son of John, do you love Me?" Peter was grieved because He said to him the third time, "Do you love Me?" And he said to Him, "Lord, You know all things; You know that I love You." Jesus said to him, "Tend My sheep." *(John 21:15-17)*

### *Reflecting* on the Word

The work that Jesus called Peter to do was the work of shepherding the flock of God. It would be hard work. Lowly work. Sometimes even dangerous work. It took a special person to do it. Certainly not a person who was in it for the money. Or one who was in it for the recognition. Or the power.

There could be only one motivation. Love.

Not a love for the open fields. Not a love for shepherding. Not even a love for the sheep. It had to be more than that. It had to be a love for the Shepherd Himself. Everything had to come from there. Every sermon. Every counseling session. Every communion. Every prayer for the sick. Every search for someone who was lost. Every correction for someone who was wayward. Every leading of the congregation to a place of pasturage. All of the work, even the lowliest part of it, had to come from there.

For three-and-a-half years Jesus has shown Peter how to do that work.

Even now He is showing him, in the way that He forgives, and to the extent that He restores.

Ken Gire

### *Responding* to the Word

I turn to you.

163

And I see, hear, feel what love is all about.

Love in the hand stretched out

to the paralysed man, to the leprosy sufferer, in healing.

Love offered to the corrupt tax official, and to Mary Magdalene.

In restoration.

Love in story and parable.

In rebuke.

Love in the stable.

Love on the cross.

Love forgiving as the pain of the nails

rasped through the body hanging there.

Love in the resurrection. . . .

Love for me.

Eddie Askew
*A Silence and a Shouting*

### *Reading* the Word

Then they returned to Jerusalem from the mount called Olivet, which is near Jerusalem, a Sabbath day's journey away. And when they had entered, they went up to the upper room, where they were staying; that is, Peter and John and James and Andrew, Philip and Thomas, Bartholomew and Matthew, James the son of Alphaeus, and Simon the Zealot, and Judas the son of James. These all with one mind were continually devoting themselves to prayer, along with the women, and Mary the mother of Jesus, and with His brothers. *(Acts 1:12-14)*

164

### *Reflecting* on the Word

Prayer is the language of the Christian community. In prayer the nature of the community becomes visible because in prayer we direct ourselves to the one who forms the community. We do not pray to each other, but together we pray to God, who calls us and makes us into a new people. Praying is not one of the many things the community does. Rather, it is its very being. Many discussions about prayer do not take this very seriously. Sometimes it seems as if the Christian community is "so busy" with its projects and plans that there is neither the time nor the mood to pray. But when prayer is no longer its primary concern, and when its many activities are no longer seen and experienced as part of prayer itself, the community quickly degenerates into a club with a common cause but no common vocation.

Henri Nouwen
*Reaching Out*

### *Responding* to the Word

O Lord, look with mercy upon this congregation of your people, drawn together from every part of the earth, united in the worship of our Lord, divided by diversities of gifts; differences of custom, usage, and tradition and loyalties of language and nation. Grant us grace fitly to be joined together, to be obedient to your will and to serve one another with our several gifts. Enrich our common life through our diversities, and help us to keep the unity of the spirit in the bond of peace. May we by your mercy listen to each other in humility, and learn from each other with patience and diligence, so that our love may grow in all knowledge and discernment. Give us a sense of gratitude to all who serve us, and who give us the comfort and leisure for study by their special labors, so that we may not forget to bestow the more abundant honor upon those members of our community whose work is less obvious or apparent. This we ask through him who was among us as one who served.

Reinhold Niebuhr
*Justice and Mercy*

### *Reading* the Word

Now when they heard this, they were cut to the quick, and they began gnashing their teeth at [Stephen]. But being full of the Holy Spirit, he gazed intently into heaven and saw the glory of God, and Jesus standing at the right hand of God; and he said, "Behold, I see the heavens opened up and the Son of Man standing at the right hand of God." But they cried out with a loud voice, and covered their ears, and they rushed upon him with one impulse. And when they had driven him out of the city, they began stoning him, and the witnesses laid aside their robes at the feet of a young man named Saul. And they went on stoning Stephen as he called upon the Lord and said, "Lord Jesus, receive my spirit!" And falling on his knees, he cried out with a loud voice, "Lord, do not hold this sin against them!" And having said this, he fell asleep. *(Acts 7:54-60)*

### *Reflecting* on the Word

I am standing upon the seashore. A ship at my side spreads her white sails to the morning breeze and starts for the blue ocean. She is an object of beauty and strength, and I stand and watch her until at length she hangs like a speck of white cloud just where the sea and sky come down to mingle with each other. Then someone at my side says: "There! She's gone." Gone where? Gone from my sight—that is all. She is just as large in mast and hull and spar as she was when she left my side, and

166

just as able to bear her load of living freight to the place of destination. Her diminished size is in me, not in her; and just at the moment when someone at my side says, "There! She's gone," there are other eyes watching her coming, and other voices ready to take up the glad shout, "There she comes!"

And that is Dying!

Author Unknown

### *Responding* to the Word

To those who are tried by the tempest, you are the calm harbour;
you are the object of all that hope.
To those who are sick, you are health;
you guide the blind and give help to those in need.
To those who face suffering, you always grant mercy,
you are a light in darkness, a place of rest for the weary. . . .
I ask you, Lord, do not count me unworthy of the suffering
that has been endured by my brothers.
Allow me to share the crown with them.
Allow us to be together in glory as we have been together in prison.
Allow me to find my rest with them, as we have confessed your
glorious name together.

167

Severus of Thrace
*Prayers of the Martyrs*
compiled and translated
by Duane W.H. Arnold

### *Reading* the Word

Now there was a certain man named Simon, who formerly was practicing magic in the city . . . of Samaria. . . . But when [the Samaritans] believed Philip preaching the good news about the kingdom of God and the name of Jesus Christ, they were being baptized, men and women alike. And even Simon himself believed; and after being baptized, he continued on with Philip; and as he observed signs and great miracles taking place, he was constantly amazed.

Now when the apostles in Jerusalem heard that Samaria had received the word of God, they sent them Peter and John, who came down and prayed for them, that they might receive the Holy Spirit. Now when Simon saw that the Spirit was bestowed through the laying on of the apostles' hands, he offered them money, saying, "Give this authority to me as well, so that everyone on whom I lay my hands may receive the Holy Spirit." But Peter said to him, "May your silver perish with you, because you thought you could obtain the gift of God with money! You have no part or portion in this matter, for your heart is not right before God." *(Acts 8:9-21)*

### *Reflecting* on the Word

If in our early Christian search we pour forth glib and ready answers, in later years we dare not do so. With the earthly loss of two grandchildren still vivid to me, I know there are no easy, simple answers as to why some are healed in this life and some are not.

But we have learned that God's objective is whole men, wholly dependent on Him. So His Spirit will counteract each time we try to tag, categorize, and pigeonhole Him—for instance, in the direction of rules for healing. Obviously, we are to worship Him rather than a set of spiritual laws.

We resist that because laws are pat and predictable, whereas people are not. Since this is true with human persons, then how much more so with God!

Even as Jesus advised us to begin by taking the lowest seat at banquets, so with healing we are well advised to begin with the lowest place. . . . "Lord, what would You like to tell me about this situation? How do You want me to pray? What do You want me to do?"

Relinquishment and such a seeking prayer will always bring His response. Often it is a surprising response that we could not possibly have anticipated.

Catherine Marshall

*Something More*

169

### *Responding* to the Word

Lord, what would You like to tell me about this situation?
How do You want me to pray?
What do You want me to do?

## *Reading* the Word

Therefore we have been buried with Him through baptism into death, in order that as Christ was raised from the dead through the glory of the Father, so we too might walk in newness of life. *(Romans 6:4)*

## *Reflecting* on the Word

Did you ever think, when you were a child, what fun it would be if your toys could come to life? Well suppose you could really have brought them to life. Imagine turning a tin soldier into a real little man. It would involve turning the tin into flesh. And suppose the tin soldier did not like it. He is not interested in flesh; all he sees is that the tin is being spoilt. He thinks you are killing him. . . .

What you would have done about that tin soldier I do not know. But what God did about us was this. The Second Person in God, the Son, became human Himself: was born into the world as an actual man. . . .

The result of this was that you now had one man who really was what all men were intended to be. . . . He chose an earthly career which involved the killing of His human desires at every turn—poverty, misunderstanding from His own family, betrayal by one of His intimate friends, being jeered at and manhandled by the Police, and execution by torture. And then, after being thus killed—killed every day in a sense—the human creature in Him, because it was united to the divine Son, came to life again. The Man in Christ rose again: not only the God. That is the whole point. For the first time we saw a real man. One tin soldier—real tin, just like the rest—had come fully and splendidly alive.

C.S. Lewis

*Mere Christianity*

### *Responding* to the Word

You say in your Word that I have been predestined to become conformed to the likeness of Christ. It sounds almost like a fairy tale, but if your Word is true, then that happily-ever-after ending is true, too. Thank you for that, Lord.

But for now, in the not-so-happy middle of the story, I have to tell you, the process is so slow . . . so frustrating . . . so painful.

A part of me remains tin while a part of me is turning into flesh. A part of me gets bent while a part of me bruises. A part of me rusts while a part of me bleeds. Sometimes I think I'd rather just polish the tin exterior, oil the joints, and just leave it at that.

Yet in my heart of hearts, Jesus is what I want to become like. So no matter how much I creak and complain, keep changing that tin soldier . . . until at last he is fully and splendidly alive.

Ken Gire

### *Reading* the Word

The wishing is present in me, but the doing of good is not. For the good that I wish, I do not do; but I practice the very evil that I do not wish. *(Romans 7:18-19)*

### *Reflecting* on the Word

Alcoholics Anonymous or A. A. is the name of a group of men and women who acknowledge that addiction to alcohol is ruining their lives. Their purpose in coming together is to give it up and help others do the same. They realize they can't pull this off by themselves. . . .

Nobody lectures them, and they do not lecture each other. They simply tell their stories with the candor that anonymity makes possible. They tell where they went wrong and how day by day they are trying to go right. They tell where they find the strength and understanding and hope to keep trying. Sometimes one of them will take special responsibility for another—to be available at any hour of day or night if the need arises. There's not much more to it than that, and it seems to be enough. Healing happens. Miracles are made.

You can't help thinking that something like this is what the Church is meant to be and maybe once was before it got to be Big Business. Sinners Anonymous. . . .

No matter what far place alcoholics end up in, either in this country or virtually anywhere else, they know that there will be

172

an A. A. meeting nearby to go to and that at that meeting they will find strangers who are not strangers to help and to heal, to listen to the truth and to tell it. . . .

Would it ever occur to Christians in a far place to turn to a Church nearby in hope of finding the same? Would they find it? If not, you wonder what is so Big about the Church's Business.

Frederick Buechner
*Whistling in the Dark*

### *Responding* to the Word

What's wrong with the people in church? . . .
They don't seem to enjoy themselves or talk to anyone.
They freeze up tight. I know because I've been watching them.
They look like penguins standing on the shore and staring at
the weary ocean. . . .
I see them waiting for a miracle when the preacher says his piece,
his one precious capsule that's supposed to save their lives for
one more week. . . .
Will the people in church ever change? Will they?

A teenager's prayer
quoted in *For Mature Adults Only*
by Norman C. Habel

### *Reading* the Word

And we know that God causes all things to work together for good to those who love God, to those who are called according to His purpose. *(Romans 8:28)*

### *Reflecting* on the Word

174

He promised that all things work together for good for those who love Him. That doesn't mean that all things that happen to us are good, but they work for good, if we let them. . . . It's something like baking a cake from scratch. All kinds of things go into it. Flour. Baking powder. Eggs. Milk. Butter. Sugar. When all those things get stirred up and put in the oven, then you have a cake. . . . Not all of the ingredients that go into a cake taste good. Some we would never choose to eat by themselves. Who would want to eat a mouthful of flour or a raw egg? If we had our choice, we'd probably just pick the milk and sugar, the sweet things. But that would never make a cake, would it?

Ken Gire

*Treasure in an Oatmeal Box*

### *Responding* to the Word

O God, who has promised that all things will work together for good to those that love you, grant us patience amidst the tumults, pains and afflictions of life, and faith to discern your love, within, above, and beyond the impartial destinies of this great drama of life. Save us from every vainglorious pretension by which we demand favors which violate your love for all your children, and grant us grace to appropriate every fortune, both good and evil, for the triumph of the suffering, crucified, and risen Lord in our souls and lives. In whose name we ask it.

Reinhold Niebuhr

*Justice and Mercy*

175

### *Reading* the Word

Be devoted to one another in brotherly love; give preference to one another in honor . . . contributing to the needs of the saints, practicing hospitality. *(Romans 12:10, 13)*

### *Reflecting* on the Word

Hospitality is not to change people, but to offer them space where change can take place. It is not to bring men and women over to our side, but to offer freedom not disturbed by dividing lines. It is not to lead our neighbor into a corner where there are no alternatives left, but to open a wide spectrum of options for choice and commitment. It is not an educated intimidation with good books, good stories and good works, but the liberation of fearful hearts so that words can find roots and bear ample fruit. . . . The paradox of hospitality is that it wants to create emptiness where strangers can enter and discover themselves as created free; free to sing their own songs, speak their own languages, dance their own dances; free also to leave and follow their own vocations. Hospitality is not a subtle invitation to adopt the life style of the host, but the gift of a chance for the guest to find his own. . . .

To convert hostility to hospitality requires the creation of the friendly empty space where we can reach out to our fellow human beings and invite them to a new relationship. This conversion is an inner event that cannot be manipulated but must

176

develop from within. Just as we cannot force a plant to grow but can take away the weeds and stones which prevent its development, so we cannot force anyone to such a personal and intimate change of heart, but we can offer a space where such a change can take place.

Henri Nouwen
*Reaching Out*

### *Responding* to the Word

Help me, O God,

To be a gracious host to anyone and everyone you send into my life.

Help me in my relationships with people to create a safe place for
    them, a place where they can lay down their burdens and find rest,

a place where they can breathe freely and deeply and simply be,

a place where they can express themselves without fear of criticism,

where they can share not just their faith but their doubts,

not just their joys but their sorrows,

not just their peace but their frustrations.

Create in me such confidence in your Spirit

that I would give Him room to work,

that I would let some things go unsaid so that He might have a
    chance to speak,

that I would respect the work He is doing in another person's life,

take off my shoes and step lightly . . . for it is holy ground.

Ken Gire

177

### *Reading* the Word

We speak God's wisdom in a mystery, the hidden wisdom, which God predestined before the ages to our glory; the wisdom which none of the rulers of this age has understood; for if they had understood it, they would not have crucified the Lord of glory; but just as it is written, "Things which eye has not seen and ear has not heard, and which have not entered the heart of man, all that God has prepared for those who love Him." *(1 Corinthians 2:7-9)*

178

### *Reflecting* on the Word

Aslan turned to them and said: "You do not yet look so happy as I mean you to be."

Lucy said: "We're so afraid of being sent away, Aslan. And you have sent us back into our own world so often."

"No fear of that," said Aslan. "Have you not guessed?"

Their hearts leaped and a wild hope rose within them.

"There was a real railway accident," said Aslan softly. "Your father and mother and all of you are—as you used to call it in the Shadow-Lands—dead. The term is over: the holidays have begun. The dream is ended: this is the morning."

And as He spoke He no longer looked to them like a lion; but the things that began to happen after that were so great and beautiful that I cannot write them. And for us this is the end of all the stories, and we can most truly say that they all lived happily ever after. But for them it was only the beginning of the real story. All their life in this world and all their adventures in Narnia had only been the cover and the title page: now at last they were beginning Chapter One of the Great Story, which no one on earth has read: which goes on for ever: in which every chapter is better than the one before.

C.S. Lewis
*The Last Battle*

### *Responding* to the Word

179

Dear God,
Help me to see that my life here on earth is just the night
    before Christmas,
and that when I awake in heaven, it will be Christmas morning.
The once-empty stockings
now bulging.
The once-hidden presents
now under the tree, waiting to be unwrapped. The holiday meal
    once waiting to be cooked
now on the table, waiting to be eaten.
Here, the dream
of sugar plums.
There, the awakening
to the wide-eyed wonder of all you have prepared for us. . . .

Ken Gire

### *Reading* the Word

Do you not know that a little leaven leavens the whole lump of dough? *(1 Corinthians 5:6)*

### *Reflecting* on the Word

In hell everything begins with little innocuous things. The history of the world began with an insignificant grab for an apple. In ordinary speech one would never think of calling it stealing, but probably only "rigging" or "cutting corners," and yet Cain's murder of his brother, the building of the tower of Babel, wars and rumors of wars are all related to these little manipulations. A murder begins with the slender, silken fibers of a few thoughts, quite internal, naturally, and well concealed in the precincts of the heart where thoughts have their privileged freedom and nobody can be forbidden to think. And adultery begins with a glance. And the bonds of the greatest passions were once but silken threads. Just as that which at first hardly moves the balance finally tips the scales in the Last Judgment, so the delicate web of trivialities becomes a closely woven net of ropes in which the Accuser seeks to catch us and bring us as spoils to the Last Judgment.

Helmut Thielicke

*Life Can Begin Again*

180

### *Responding* to the Word

It was Benjamin Franklin, I think, Lord, who said:
"For the want of a nail the shoe was lost,
For the want of a shoe the horse was lost,
For the want of a horse the rider was lost,
For the want of a rider the battle was lost,
For the want of a battle the kingdom was lost—
All for the want of a horseshoe-nail."

Help me to see how essential little things are to the kingdom of God, how the battles for the human heart are won or lost over such things. Grant me the grace of your Holy Spirit's conviction about those little things. For the sake of my heart and the greater sake of your kingdom, I pray. Amen.

Ken Gire

### *Reading* the Word

If I speak with the tongues of men and of angels, but do not have love, I have become a noisy gong or a clanging cymbal. And if I have the gift of prophecy, and know all mysteries and all knowledge; and if I have all faith, so as to remove mountains, but do not have love, I am nothing. And if I give all my possessions to feed the poor, and I deliver my body to be burned, but do not have love, it profits me nothing. *(1 Corinthians 13:1-3)*

### *Reflecting* on the Word

182

The relation to any particular injunction to the whole life of the soul is the relationship, I think, of the artist to the particular rules and laws that govern what he is doing. Take, for example, the realm of music. A man may play a piece of great music quite accurately; he may make no mistakes at all. And yet it may be true to say of him that he did not really play Beethoven's Moonlight Sonata. He played the notes correctly, but not the Sonata. What was he doing? He was mechanically striking the right notes, but missing the soul and the real interpretation. He wasn't doing what Beethoven intended and meant.

D. Martyn Lloyd-Jones
*Studies in the Sermon on the Mount*

### *Responding* to the Word

I confess, Lord, that so many times I hit the right notes on the keyboard but miss the soul of what you have given me to play.

How often I give, but not cheerfully. How often I serve, but not willingly. How often I speak, but not sincerely. How often I show up for things, for church, for a friend, for a family member, and yet my heart isn't in it.

Maybe because it makes me feel good about myself, or maybe because it makes me look good in other people's eyes. I'm not sure. But I am sure of this. So many of the things I do, even the things I do for you, are done if not without love then certainly without enough love.

183

Reading my Bible. Praying for other people. Volunteering for something. So often these are just items on my To-Do List that I dutifully check off when they're done. So often I just rotely pound out the moments of my day, without thought, without feeling.

To the untrained ear, my life may sound pretty good. At least all the notes have been touched. And in the proper order.

How does it all sound to you, God? As you look at the sheet music of my daily schedule, is it music to your ears? Or is it just so much noise?

Help me, O God, to so live my life that what is played is not just a succession of correct notes, but a Sonata.

Ken Gire

### *Reading* the Word

You are our letter, written in our hearts, known and read by all men, being manifested that you are a letter of Christ, cared for by us, written not with ink, but with the Spirit of the living God. . . . *(2 Corinthians 3:2-3)*

### *Reflecting* on the Word

This is the universal spirit which pervades every heart, speaking to each one individually. It speaks through Isaiah, Jeremiah, Ezekiel. Without knowing it, all are instruments of that spirit to bring the message ever freshly to the world. And if souls knew how to unite themselves to this purpose, their lives would be a succession of divine scriptures, continuing till the end of time, not written with ink on paper, but on each human heart. This is what the book of life is about. Unlike the holy scriptures, it will not be a history of the work of the Holy Spirit over the centuries since the world began to the day of judgement. In it will be written down every thought, word, deed and suffering of all souls. And that scripture will then be a complete record of divine action.

And so the sequel to the New Testament is being written now, by action and suffering. Saintly souls are in the succession of the prophets and the Apostles, not by writing canonical books, but by continuing the history of divine purpose with their lives, those moments are so many syllables and sentences through which it is vividly expressed. The books the Holy Spirit is writing are living, and every soul a volume in which the divine author makes a true revelation of his word, explaining it to every heart, unfolding it in every moment.

Jean-Pierre De Caussade
*The Sacrament of the Present Moment*

## *Responding* to the Word

*After a four months' refugee Bible class in which a number of illiterate women had learned to read, the day came when they were returning to their homes. At the meeting before parting one of the women prayed:*

185

We are going home to many who cannot read. So, Lord, make us Bibles so that those who cannot read the Book can read it in us.

*The World at One in Prayer*
edited by Daniel J. Fleming

### *Reading* the Word

As servants of God we commend ourselves in every way: in great endurance; in troubles, hardships and distresses; in beatings, imprisonments and riots; in hard work, sleepless nights and hunger; in purity, understanding, patience and kindness; in the Holy Spirit and in sincere love; in truthful speech and in the power of God; with weapons of righteousness in the right hand and in the left . . . having nothing, and yet possessing everything. *(2 Corinthians 6:4-7, 10, NIV)*

186

### *Reflecting* on the Word

I once saw a very beautiful picture: it was a landscape at evening. In the distance on the right-hand side a row of hills appeared blue in the evening mist. Above those hills the splendour of the sunset, the grey clouds with their linings of silver and gold and purple. The landscape is a plain or heath covered with grass and its yellow leaves, for it was autumn. Through the landscape a road leads to a high mountain far, far away, on the top of that mountain is a city whereon the setting sun casts a glory. On the road walks a pilgrim, staff in hand. He has been walking for a good long while already and he is very tired. And now he meets a woman, or figure in black, that makes one think of St. Paul's word: As being sorrowful yet always rejoicing. That Angel of God has been placed there to encourage the pilgrims and to answer their questions and the pilgrim asks her: "Does the road go uphill then all the way?"

And the answer is: "Yes to the very end."

And he asks again: "And will the journey take all day long?"

And the answer is: "From morn till night my friend."

And the pilgrim goes on sorrowful yet always rejoicing—sorrowful because it is so far off and the road is long. Hopeful as he looks up to the eternal city far away, resplendent in the evening glow. . . .

And he says: "I shall be more and more tired but also nearer and nearer to Thee."

Vincent van Gogh

*from a sermon he preached in 1877*

187

### *Responding* to the Word

I thank Thee that this Christian way whereon I walk is not untried or uncharted road, but a road beaten hard by the footsteps of saints, apostles, prophets, and martyrs. I thank Thee for the finger-posts and danger-signals with which it is marked at every turning and which may be known to me through the study of the Bible. . . .

When the way seems dark before me, give me grace to walk trustingly: when much is obscure to me, let me be all the more faithful to the little I can clearly see: when the distant scene is clouded, let me rejoice that at least the next step is plain. . . .

John Baillie

*A Diary of Private Prayer*

## *Reading* the Word

For by grace you have been saved through faith; and that not of yourselves, it is the gift of God; not as a result of works, that no one should boast. *(Ephesians 2:8-9)*

## *Reflecting* on the Word

When I think of grace, I think of a figure skater axeling in the air and shaving ice on the way down. I think of Fred Astaire dancing. Of snowflakes falling. Of Daryl Strawberry looping a homerun into the centerfield stands. I think of Beethoven's sixth symphony, "The Pastoral," especially the few sprinkling moments before the storm and the few sun-washed ones after it. I think of shade clouds parasoling by on a sultry, summer afternoon. And flyfishing in Cheeseman Canyon. I think of translucent waves curling toward a lonely, sand beach. I think of the birds of the air, the flowers of the field.

And I think of Jesus. Especially Jesus.

Full of grace and truth is how John thought of Him. I think of Him that way, too, especially when I hear Him telling the woman caught in adultery, "Neither do I condemn you. Go your way and sin no more." I think of Him washing the disciples' feet. Of Him praying on the cross, "Father, forgive them for they know not what they do." Of Him restoring Peter with the commission to "Feed My sheep." And grace seems the only word regal enough to drape around His shoulders.

188

I don't know your heart. But I know mine. And I know how desperately it needs grace. Not just to get me to heaven . . . but to get me through the day.

Ken Gire

## *Responding* to the Word

Amazing grace! how sweet the sound,
That saved a wretch like me!
I once was lost, but now am found,
Was blind, but now I see.

'Twas grace that taught my heart to fear,
And grace my fears relieved;
How precious did that grace appear
The hour I first believed!

Through many dangers, toils and snares,
I have already come;
'Tis grace that brought me safe thus far.
And grace will lead me home.

*"Amazing Grace! How Sweet the Sound"*
lyrics by John Newton, 1725-1807
music by Edwin O. Exceil, 1851-1921

189

### *Reading* the Word

And do not get drunk with wine, for that is dissipation, but be filled with the Spirit. *(Ephesians 5:18)*

### *Reflecting* on the Word

Let us imagine we see two fountains with basins which fill with water. . . . These two basins are filled in different ways; the one with water from a distance, flowing into it through many pipes and waterworks, while the other basin is built near the source of the spring itself and fills quite noiselessly. If the fountain is plentiful, like the one we speak of, after the basin is full the water overflows in a great stream which flows continually. There is no need here of any machinery, nor does the water run through aqueducts. . . .

The water running through the aqueducts seems like sensible devotion, which is obtained through meditation. We gain it by our thoughts, by meditating on created things, and by the labour of our minds; in short, it is the result of our endeavours, and so makes the commotion I spoke of, while bringing profit to the soul. The other fountain is like diving consolations; it receives the water from the source itself which signifies God; as usual, when His Majesty wills to bestow on us any peace, calm, and sweetness in the inmost depths of our being, I know neither where nor how.

St. Teresa of Avila
quoted in *The Soul Afire*
edited by H.A. Reinhold

## *Responding* to the Word

O Holy Spirit, omnipresent, free,
I bring the only thing I really have,
An empty vessel, to be filled by Thee.

I open wide the windows of my soul:
Thy light and love pour in to make me whole,
Fill me with wisdom and make clear the way,
Fill me with love for all I meet this day,
Fill me with patience when the way seems long,
Fill me with joy and with a gladsome song. . . .

Let all the good so fill and overflow
That all the world may share it as I go.

Ralph O'Day

quoted from *Prayers for Daily Living*

### *Reading* the Word

Have this attitude in yourselves which was also in Christ Jesus, who, although He existed in the form of God, did not regard equality with God a thing to be grasped, but emptied Himself, taking the form of a bondservant, and being made in the likeness of men. And being found in appearance as a man, He humbled Himself by becoming obedient to the point of death, even death on a cross. Therefore also God highly exalted Him, and bestowed on Him the name which is above every name, that at the name of Jesus every knee should bow, of those who are in heaven, and on earth, and under the earth, and that every tongue should confess that Jesus Christ is Lord, to the glory of God the Father. *(Philippians 2:5-11)*

### *Reflecting* on the Word

The love of God [has] become visible in Jesus. How is that love made visible through Jesus? It is made visible in the descending way. That is the great mystery of the Incarnation. God has descended to us human beings to become a human being with us; and once among us, descended to the total dereliction of one condemned to death. It isn't easy really to feel and understand from the inside this descending way of Jesus. Every fiber of our being rebels against it. We don't mind paying attention to poor people from time to time; but descending to a state of poverty and becoming poor with the

192

poor, that we don't want to do. And yet that is the way Jesus chose as the way to know God.

Henri Nouwen
*Show Me the Way*

### *Responding* to the Word

Let me learn by paradox
that the way down is up,
that the way to be low is to be high,
that the broken heart is the healed heart,
that the contrite spirit is the rejoicing spirit,
that the repenting soul is the victorious soul,
that to have nothing is to possess all,
that to bear the cross is to wear the crown,
that to give is to receive,
that the valley is the place of vision. . . .

Arthur Bennett
*The Valley of Vision*

193

## *Reading* the Word

Fathers, do not exasperate your children, that they may not lose heart. *(Colossians 3:21)*

## *Reflecting* on the Word

If children live with criticism, they learn to condemn.
If children live with hostility, they learn to fight.
If children live with fear, they learn to be apprehensive.
If children live with pity, they learn to feel sorry for themselves.
If children live with ridicule, they learn to be shy.
If children live with jealousy, they learn what envy is.
If children live with shame, they learn to feel guilty.
If children live with tolerance, they learn to be patient.
If children live with encouragement, they learn to be confident.
If children live with praise, they learn to appreciate.
If children live with approval, they learn to like themselves.
If children live with acceptance, they learn to find love in
    the world.
If children live with recognition, they learn to have a goal.
If children live with sharing, they learn to be generous.
If children live with honesty and fairness, they learn what truth
    and justice are.
If children live with security, they learn to have faith in
    themselves and in those around them.
If children live with friendliness, they learn that the world is

a nice place in which to live.

If children live with serenity, they learn to have peace of mind. . . .

Dorothy L. Nolte

### *Responding* to the Word

Oh, God, I was so cross to the children today. Forgive me.

Oh, God, I was so discouraged, so tired, and so unreasonable. I took it out on them. Forgive me.

Forgive me my bad temper, my impatience, and most of all my yelling.

I cringe to think of it. My heart aches. I want to go down on my knees beside each little bed and wake them up and beg them to forgive me. Only I can't, it would only upset them more.

I've got to go on living with the memory of this day. My unjust tirades. The guilty fear in their eyes as they flew about trying to appease me. Thinking it all their fault—my troubles, my disappointments. . . .

And all I can do now is to straighten a cover, move a toy fallen out of an upthrust hand, touch a small head burrowed into a pillow, and beg in my heart, "Forgive me."

Lord, in failing these little ones whom you've put into my keeping, I'm failing you. Please let your infinite patience and goodness fill me tomorrow. Stand by me, keep your hand on my shoulder.

Marjorie Holmes
*I've Got to Talk to Somebody, God*

195

## *Reading* the Word

Pray without ceasing. *(1 Thessalonians 5:17)*

## *Reflecting* on the Word

How in the world can we possibly "pray without ceasing," or "pray continually"?

Does this mean you can't read a book or a newspaper because you have to be praying instead? Does it mean you can do nothing else at all but pray? To look at it this way would be to make that command an impossibility. However, I do believe it is something that does have meaning. It seems to me that this command means that we are to be constantly so conscious of God's existence and so aware of His presence, that there is a very short gap between a sudden need of speaking to the Lord, and our actually speaking to Him. I feel it means that we are walking so close to the reality of His being with us that we naturally talk to Him (in our minds, of course) when we are in the dentist's chair, in the waiting room of a doctor's or lawyer's office, out on a tractor, waiting for a plane or bus, talking to someone who has just had a shock. Whether it is a brief time of prayer or a long, long one, the atmosphere of the normality of talking to God is what I feel is meant by the command to "pray continually."

Edith Schaeffer

*Common Sense Christian Living*

196

### *Responding* to the Word

Lord,

I remember Edith Schaeffer once saying that prayer should be as natural as breathing and as necessary as air. To me that captures the essence of what it means to pray without ceasing. I want so much to live like that, Lord. I want my life to be sustained by the steady rhythms of prayer, by the constant in-breathing and out-breathing of a soul that is not only alive to you but aware of its moment-by-moment dependence on you.

With every awareness of a need . . . let me breathe out a petition.
With every awareness of someone else's need . . . intercession.
With every awareness of sin . . . confession.
With every awareness of sin against me . . . forgiveness.
With every awareness of you . . . praise.
With every awareness of your gifts . . . gratitude.

Ken Gire

## *Reading* the Word

In everything give thanks; for this is God's will for you in Christ Jesus. *(1 Thessalonians 5:18)*

## *Reflecting* on the Word

Jacob looked down at his path as if it were the current of a great river. As he stared into the flow he saw the seemingly unending line of moments given to him. Then, like a man marking a trail, he began to put his prayer between the moments, making the common profound by pausing.

198

Using prayer to tie knots in time, Jacob isolated the details that would pass before others as a stream of events.

In this way Jacob secured the moments in his life, returned their individuality, allowed the luster in each of them to be observed, and, appreciated and saved, transformed his moments into a string of pearls.

Jacob the Baker
in Noah ben Shea's *Jacob's Journey*

### *Responding* to the Word

Lord, thank you for each moment,
for the holy moment,
the music,
the child's eyes,
for the sunlight,
the touch,
the tears,
for the trembling pleasure,
the unutterable beauty,
the breathing,
for the life and love and heart in me, aware,
and the wholeness spreading in me.
Touch me
through whatever comes as a gift
that I may be graceful
and praise you in it all.

Ted Loder
*Guerrillas of Grace*

## *Reading* the Word

I want the men in every place to pray, lifting up holy hands. . . .
*(1 Timothy 2:8)*

## *Reflecting* on the Word

The resistance to praying is like the resistance of tightly clenched fists. This image shows a tension, a desire to cling tightly to yourself, a greediness which betrays fear. A story about an elderly woman brought to a psychiatric center exemplifies this attitude. She was wild, swinging at everything in sight, and frightening everyone so much that the doctors had to take everything away from her. But there was one small coin which she gripped in her fist and would not give up. In fact, it took two people to pry open that clenched hand. It was as though she would lose her very self along with the coin. If they deprived her of that last possession, she would have nothing more and be nothing more. That was her fear.

When you are invited to pray, you are asked to open your tightly clenched fist and give up your last coin. . . .

To pray means to open your hands before God. It means slowly relaxing the tension which squeezes your hands together and accepting your existence with an increasing readiness, not as a possession to defend, but as a gift to receive.

Henri Nouwen
*With Open Hands*

200

### *Responding* to the Word

Dear God,
I am so afraid to open my clenched fists!
Who will I be when I have nothing left to hold on to?
Who will I be when I stand before you with my empty hands?
Please help me to gradually open my hands
and to discover that I am not what I own,
but what you want to give me.
And what you want to give me is love,
unconditional, everlasting love.

Henri Nouwen     201
*With Open Hands*

### *Reading* the Word

But godliness actually is a means of great gain, when accompanied by contentment. For we have brought nothing into the world, so we cannot take anything out of it either. And if we have food and covering, with these we shall be content.
*(1 Timothy 6:6-8)*

### *Reflecting* on the Word

As I sat there, tasting brown bread with lettuce, tomato, and bacon, and turned my mind to being content—actively content with flavor—I looked at the rocks at my elbow. I examined carefully the wonder of tiny fern and the perfection of minute lavender and pink flowers growing out of the crevices. Then I listened with attention to the bird songs and the sounds of splashing water against the rocks. I took the time to be really aware of the smell of fragrant honeysuckle and I thought of the reality of being actively content as a command.

You and I are to really learn to be content. We need to practice this as we would practice the scales on the piano. It came to me that an active contentment is a moment-by-moment practice, not a big sweeping thing. The major ingredient of contentment is not necessarily some overwhelming emotional or spiritual experience, after which one is always content, no matter what. The raw materials which bring about contentment are a varied, diverse number of things, differing from moment to

202

moment, hour to hour, day to day. It is the active noticing of what we have been given in any one moment to enjoy which brings the active result of contentment.

Edith Schaeffer

*Affliction*

### *Responding* to the Word

Lord, may your kingdom come into my heart to sanctify me, nourish me and purify me. How insignificant is the passing moment to the eye without faith! But how important each moment is to the eye enlightened by faith! How can we deem insignificant anything which has been caused by you? Every moment and every event is guided by you, and so contains your infinite greatness.

So, Lord, I glorify you in everything that happens to me. In whatever manner you make me live and die, I am content. Events please me for their own sake, regardless of their consequences, because your action lies behind them. Everything is heaven to me because all my moments manifest your love.

Jean-Pierre De Caussade

*Book of Prayers*

compiled by Robert Van de Weyer

203

### *Reading* the Word

Abraham trusted God, and when God told him to leave home and go far away to another land which he promised to give him, Abraham obeyed. Away he went, not even knowing where he was going. And even when he reached God's promised land, he lived in tents like a mere visitor, as did Isaac and Jacob, to whom God gave the same promise. Abraham did this because he was confidently waiting for God to bring him to that strong heavenly city whose designer and builder is God. *(Hebrews 11:8-10, TLB)*

204

### *Reflecting* on the Word

We don't like risk, and even though the frontiers of spiritual growth require it, we prefer to avoid it. Not only would we like to have the frontiers of the spirit scouted out for us, we would also like to have the frontier fully tamed and settled, like a new suburban development with well-lighted streets and sewers installed, established zoning codes, houses built and finished save for seeding the lawn and planting the shrubs, shopping centers nearby, and adequate police protection. No pioneering for us—no danger from the dark wild, no felling trees or clearing boulders so that we can plant a subsistence garden, no climbing mountain passes or fording swollen streams. We prefer comfortable safety to risk.

The spiritual world, however, cannot be made suburban. It is always the frontier, and if we would live in it, we must accept and even rejoice that it remains untamed.

Howard Macy
*Rhythms of the Inner Life*

### *Responding* to the Word

O Lord, my Lord, I am a stranger in a strange land. Absent are all the subtleties of custom and language and sight and smell and taste which normally give me my bearings.

Jesus, everliving Teacher, use my out-of-placeness to remind me again of my alien status in this world. I belong to another kingdom and live out of another reality. May I always be ultimately concerned to learn the nuances of this eternal reality so that when it becomes my permanent residence I will not find it strange in the least.

In the name of him who entered a foreign land so that whosoever will might come home to that for which they were created. Amen.

Richard Foster
*Prayers from the Heart*
(a prayer composed during a lengthy stay in Southeast Asia)

### *Reading* the Word

All these died in faith, without receiving the promises, but having seen them and having welcomed them from a distance, and having confessed that they were strangers and exiles on the earth. *(Hebrews 11:13)*

### *Reflecting* on the Word

Most of the great figures of the Old Testament died without ever seeing the fulfillment of the promises they relied on. Paul expended himself building the early church, but as his life drew to a close he could see only a string of tiny outposts along the Mediterranean, many weakened by fleshly indulgence or divided over doctrinal disputes.

In more recent times, the great colonial pastor Cotton Mather prayed for revival several hours each day for twenty years; the Great Awakening began the year he died. The British Empire finally abolished slavery as the Christian parliamentarian and abolitionist leader William Wilberforce lay on his deathbed, exhausted from his nearly fifty-year campaign against the practice of human bondage. Few were the converts during Hudson Taylor's lifelong mission work in the Orient; but today millions of Chinese embrace the faith he so patiently planted and tended.

Some might think this divine pattern cruel, but I am convinced there is a sovereign wisdom to it. Knowing how susceptible we are to success's siren call, God does not allow us to see, and therefore glory in, what is done through us. The very nature of the obedience He demands is that it be given without regard to circumstances or results.

Charles Colson
*Loving God*

### *Responding* to the Word

O God, the Lord of all ages, who has made us the creatures of time, so that every tomorrow is an unknown country, and every decision a venture of faith, grant us, frail children of the day, who are blind to the future to move toward it with a sure confidence in your love, from which neither life nor death can separate us. . . .

You have given your children, as to Abraham, many lands of promise, periods of peace and just communities; grant that we trust not these immediate securities but that we may live therein in tents, as did Abraham; grant us grace to build our cities here on earth more soberly, because we know ourselves to be pilgrims and strangers here, desiring a better country.

Reinhold Niebuhr
*Justice and Mercy*

207

### *Reading* the Word

They were stoned, they were sawn in two, they were tempted, they were put to death with the sword; they went about in sheepskins, in goatskins, being destitute, afflicted, ill-treated (men of whom the world was not worthy), wandering in deserts and mountains and caves and holes in the ground. And all these, having gained approval through their faith, did not receive what was promised, because God had provided something better for us, so that apart from us they should not be made perfect. *(Hebrews 11:37-40)*

208

### *Reflecting* on the Word

Bonhoeffer often asked himself about the deeper meaning of his life, which seemed to him so disconnected and confused. A few months before his death, when coming events cast their shadows before, he wrote in prison: "It all depends on whether or not the fragment of our life reveals the plan and material of the whole. There are fragments which are only good to be thrown away, and others which are important for centuries to come, because their fulfillment can only be a divine work. They are fragments of necessity. If our life, however remotely, reflects such a fragment . . . we shall not have to bewail our fragmentary life, but, on the contrary, rejoice in it."

"Memoir" by G. Leibholz
in *Cost of Discipleship* by Dietrich Bonhoeffer

### *Responding* to the Word

God, grant me the
Serenity to accept the things
I cannot change;
Courage to change the things I can; and
Wisdom to know the difference.

Living one day at a time;
Enjoying one moment at a time;
Accepting hardship
As the pathway to peace.

Taking, as He did,
This sinful world as it is
not as I would have it.

Trusting that He will make
all things right
If I surrender to His will.

That I may be reasonably happy
in this life,
And supremely happy
With Him forever in the next.

Reinhold Niebuhr
*Justice and Mercy*

209

### *Reading* the Word

Every good thing bestowed and every perfect gift is from above, coming down from the Father of lights, with whom there is no variation, or shifting shadow. *(James 1:17)*

### *Reflecting* on the Word

Earthly goods are given to be used, not to be collected. In the wilderness God gave Israel the manna every day, and they had no need to worry about food and drink. Indeed, if they kept any of the manna over until the next day, it went bad. In the same way, the disciple must receive his portion from God every day. If he stores it up as a permanent possession, he spoils not only the gift, but himself as will, for he sets his heart on his accumulated wealth, and makes it a barrier between himself and God. Where our treasure is, there is our trust, our security, our consolation and our God.

Dietrich Bonhoeffer
*The Cost of Discipleship*

### *Responding* to the Word

What have we, O heavenly Father, that we have not received? Every good gift, and every perfect gift, is from above, and cometh down from thee, which art the Father of lights. Seeing, then, all that we have is thine, whether it pertain to the body or the soul, how can we be proud, and boast ourselves of that which is none of our own; seeing also that as to give, so also to take away again, thou art able and wilt, whensoever thy gifts be abused, and thou not acknowledged to be the giver of them? Take, therefore, away from me all pride and houghtiness of mind, graft in me true humility, that I may acknowledge thee the giver of all good things be thankful unto thee for them, and use them to thy glory and the profit of my neighbor. Grant also that all my glory and rejoicing may be in no earthly creatures, but in thee alone, which dost mercy equity, and righteousness upon earth. To thee alone be all glory.

211

Liturgies of King Edward VI
*One Prayer at a Time*
edited by F. Forrester Church
and Terrence J. Mulry

### *Reading* the Word

You have been distressed by various trials, that . . . your faith, being more precious than gold which is perishable, even though tested by fire, may be found to result in praise and glory and honor at the revelation of Jesus Christ. *(1 Peter 1:6-7)*

### *Reflecting* on the Word

With a strong forearm, the apron-clad blacksmith puts his tongs into the fire, grasps the heated metal, and places it on his anvil. His keen eye examines the glowing piece. He sees what the tool is now and envisions what he wants it to be—sharper, flatter, wider, longer. With a clear picture in his mind, he begins to pound. His left hand still clutching the hot mass with the tongs, the right hand slams the two-pound sledge upon the moldable metal. . . .

Wang! Wang! The hammer slams. The shop rings with noise, the air fills with smoke and the softened metal responds.

But the response doesn't come easily. It doesn't come without discomfort. To melt down the old and recast it as new is a disrupting process. Yet the metal remains on the anvil, allowing the toolmaker to remove the scars, repair the cracks, refill the voids, and purge the impurities.

And, with time, a change occurs: what was dull becomes sharpened; what was crooked becomes straight; what was weak becomes strong; and what was useless becomes valuable.

Then the blacksmith stops. He ceases his pounding and sets

212

down his hammer. With a strong left arm, he lifts the tongs until the freshly molded metal is at eye level. In the still silence he examines the smoking tool . . . for any mars or cracks.

There are none.

Now the smith enters the final stage of his task. He plunges the smoldering instrument into a nearby bucket of water. With a hiss and a rush of smoke, the metal immediately begins to harden. The heat surrenders to the onslaught of cool water and the pliable, soft mineral becomes an unbending, useful tool.

Max Lucado

*On the Anvil*　213

### *Responding* to the Word

Lay me on an anvil, O God.
Beat me and hammer me into a crowbar.
Let me pry loose old walls.
Let me lift and loosen old foundations.

Lay me on an anvil, O God.
Beat me and hammer me into a steel spike.
Drive me into the girders that hold a skyscraper together.
Take red-hot rivets and fasten me into the central girders.
Let me be the great nail holding a skyscraper through
　　blue nights into white stars.

Carl Sandburg

*The World at One in Prayer*

edited by Daniel J. Fleming

### *Reading* the Word

For this finds favor, if for the sake of conscience toward God a man bears up under sorrows when suffering unjustly. For what credit is there if, when you sin and are harshly treated, you endure it with patience? But if when you do what is right and suffer for it you patiently endure it, this finds favor with God. For you have been called for this purpose, since Christ also suffered for you, leaving you an example for you to follow in His steps, who committed no sin, nor was any deceit found in His mouth; and while being reviled, He did not revile in return; while suffering, He uttered no threats, but kept entrusting Himself to Him who judges righteously. *(1 Peter 2:19-23)*

### *Reflecting* on the Word

Don't vex your minds by trying to explain the suffering you have to endure in this life. . . .

Even in the midst of your suffering you are in his kingdom. You are always his children, and he has his protecting arm around you. . . . Don't ask why; don't try to understand. Does a child understand everything his father does? Can he comprehend parental wisdom? No—but he can confidently nestle in his father's arms and feel perfect happiness, even while tears glisten in his eyes, because he is his father's child.

Albert Schweitzer
*Reverence for Life*

## Responding to the Word

Father in heaven,

for all who watch and wait and weep;

for all who have lost heart, and are fearful of the footfall
of despair;

for those who feel that nothing matters now, and have
relaxed their watch where unrelenting temptation hides
in the shadows;

for eyes which have grown weary scanning a sailless sea for ships
which have never come in;

for those whose love has gone unrequited and whose hungry
hearts are starved;

for those who have lost the faith which once was theirs,
and voyage strange and stormy seas alone—

for all these we pray that of thy mercy thou wouldst restore
their unshepherded souls, and lead them in right paths for thy
name's sake. Amen.

Hubert L. Simpson
in *Channels of Devotion*
by Gladys C. Murrell

215

### *Reading* the Word

We know that we have passed out of death into life, because we love the brethren. He who does not love abides in death. Every one who hates his brother is a murderer; and you know that no murderer has eternal life abiding in him. *(1 John 3:14-15)*

### *Reflecting* on the Word

Hate is as all-absorbing as love, as irrational, and in its own way as satisfying. As lovers thrive on the presence of the beloved, haters revel in encounters with the one they hate. They confirm him in all their darkest suspicions. They add fuel to all his most burning animosities. The anticipation of them makes the hating heart pound. The memory of them can be as sweet as young love.

The major difference between hating and loving is perhaps that whereas to love somebody is to be fulfilled and enriched by the experience, to hate somebody is to be diminished and drained by it. Lovers, by losing themselves in their loving, find themselves, become themselves. Haters simply lose themselves. Theirs is the ultimate consuming passion.

Frederick Buechner
*Whistling in the Dark*

216

### *Responding* to the Word

God, I cannot separate
my hatred for what was done
from the person who did it.

I despise the deed.
I loathe the person who did the deed.
My rage is my only revenge.

But, God, my rage destroys me too.
I feel this seething anger
searing my own soul.

O Lord, my God,
deliver me
from the evil
I would do to myself.

Richard Foster
*Prayers from the Heart*

217

### *Reading* the Word

"I am the Alpha and the Omega," says the Lord God, "who is and who was and is to come, the Almighty." *(Revelation 1:8)*

### *Reflecting* on the Word

People who live by faith have a particularly acute sense of living "in the middle." We believe that God is at the beginning of all things, and we believe that God is at the conclusion of all life— St. John's striking epigram: "the Alpha and the Omega" (Rev. 1:8). It is routine among us to assume that the beginning was good ("and God saw everything that he had made, and behold it was very good"). It is agreed among us that the conclusion will be good ("And I saw a new heaven and a new earth"). That would seem to guarantee that everything between the good beginning and the good ending will also be good. But it doesn't turn out that way. . . . I am rejected by a parent, coerced by a government, divorced by a spouse, discriminated against by a society, injured by another's carelessness. . . . Between the believed but unremembered beginning and the hoped for but unimaginable ending there are disappointments, contradictions, not-to-be-explained absurdities, bewildering paradoxes—each of them a reversal of expectation.

Eugene Peterson
*Reversed Thunder*

### *Responding* to the Word

Oh Lord God,
I have no idea where I am going,
I do not see the road ahead of me,
I cannot know for certain where it will end.

Nor do I really know myself,
and that fact that I think I am following Your will
does not mean that I am actually doing so.
But I believe that the desire to please You
does in fact please You.
And I hope I have that desire
in all that I am doing. . . .
And I know that if I do this
You will lead me by the right road,
though I may know nothing about it.
Therefore I will trust You always
though I may seem to be lost
and in the shadow of death.
I will not fear,
for You are ever with me,
and You will never leave me
to make my journey alone.

219

Thomas Merton

quoted in *A Seven Day Journey with Thomas Merton*

by Esther de Waal

## *Reading* the Word

And he carried me away in the Spirit to a great and high mountain, and showed me the holy city, Jerusalem, coming down out of heaven from God, having the glory of God. Her brilliance was like a very costly stone, as a stone of crystal-clear jasper. It had a great and high wall, with twelve gates. . . . And the twelve gates were twelve pearls; each one of the gates was a single pearl. And the street of the city was pure gold, like transparent glass. And I saw no temple in it, for the Lord God, the Almighty, and the Lamb, are its temple. And the city has no need of the sun or of the moon to shine upon it, for the glory of God has illumined it, and its lamp is the Lamb. *(Revelation 21:10-12a, 21-23)*

## *Reflecting* on the Word

It will not be the pearly gates, nor the jasper walls, nor the streets paved with transparent gold that will make it heaven to us. These would not satisfy us. If these were all, we would not want to stay there forever. I heard of a child whose mother was very sick; and while she lay very low, one of the neighbors took the child away to stay with her until the mother should be well again. But instead of getting better, the mother died; and they thought they would not take the child home until the funeral was all over; and would never tell her about her mother being dead. So a while afterward they brought the little girl home.

First she went into the sitting room to find her mother;

then she went into the parlor to find her mother there; and she went from one end of the house to the other and could not find her. At last she said, "Where is my mama?" And when they told her mama was gone, the little thing wanted to go back to the neighbor's house again. Home had lost its attraction to her since her mother was not there any longer. No, it will not be the jasper walls and the pearly gates that will make heaven attractive. It is our being with God.

Dwight L. Moody
*Heaven*

221

## *Responding* to the Word

Bring us, O Lord God, at the last awaking into the house and gate of heaven, to enter into that gate and dwell in that house, where there shall be no darkness nor dazzling, but one equal light; no noise nor silence, but one equal music; no fear nor hopes, but an equal possession; no ends nor beginnings, but one equal eternity; in the habitations of the majesty and thy glory, world without end.

John Donne
quoted in *A Diary of Prayer*
by Elizabeth Goudge

# Acknowledgments

Reasonable care has been taken to trace ownership of the materials quoted from this book, and to obtain permission to use copyrighted materials, when necessary.

*The Cost of Discipleship*, Dietrich Bonhoeffer, 1959, Macmillan Company, New York, New York. All rights reserved.

*A Diary of Private Prayer*, John Baillie, 1977, Charles Scribner's Sons, New York, New York. All rights reserved.

*The Forever Feast*, Paul Brand, 1993, Servant Publications, Ann Arbor, Michigan. All rights reserved.

*Guerrillas of Grace*, Ted Loder, 1984, Innisfree Press, Philadelphia, Pennsylvania. All rights reserved.

*Habitation of Dragons*, Keith Miller, 1970, Word Publishing, Nashville, Tennessee. All rights reserved.

*The Helper*, Catherine Marshall, 1978, Word Publishers, Nashville, Tennessee. All rights reserved.

*How Can I Find You, God?* by Marjorie Holmes. Copyright © 1975 by Marjorie Holmes. Used by permission of Doubleday, a division of Bantam Doubleday Dell Publishing Group, Inc.

*I've Got to Talk to Somebody, God*, Marjorie Holmes, 1969, Doubleday, New York, New York. All rights reserved.

*Justice and Mercy*, Reinhold Niebuhr, 1974, Harper & Row, New York, New York. All rights reserved.

*Lament for a Son*, Nicholas Wolterstorff, 1987, William B. Eerdmans Publishing Co., Grand Rapids, Michigan. All rights reserved.

*Life Can Begin Again*, Helmut Thielicke, 1963, The Lutterworth Press, Cambridge, England. All rights reserved.

*The Magnificent Defeat*, Frederick Buechner, 1966, Harper & Row, New York, New York. All rights reserved.

*Miracle of Life*, Ken Gire, 1993, Zondervan Publishing, Grand Rapids, Michigan. All rights reserved.

*On the Anvil*, Max Lucado, 1985, Tyndale House Publishing, Carol Stream, Illinois. All rights reserved

*The Parables of Jesus*, George Buttrick, 1928, Harper & Brothers, New York, New York. All rights reserved.

*The Prayer Tree*, Michael Leunig, 1991, Collins Dove, North Blackburn, Victoria. All rights reserved.

*Prayers from the Heart*, Richard Foster, 1994, HarperCollins Publishing, New York, New York. All rights reserved.

*The Problem of Pain*, C.S. Lewis, 1962, HarperCollins Ltd, Hammersmith, London, United Kingdom. All rights reserved.

*The Pursuit of God*, A.W. Tozer, 1982, Christian Publications, Inc., Camp Hill, Pennsylvania. All rights reserved.

*Reaching Out* by Henri Nouwen. Copyright © 1975 by Henri J.M. Nouwen. Used by permission of Doubleday, a division of Bantam Doubleday Dell Publishing Group, Inc.

*Rhythms of the Inner Life*, Howard Macy, 1992, Barclay Press, Newberg, Oregon. All rights reserved

*A Room Called Remember*, Frederick Buechner, 1984, Harper & Row, New York, New York. All rights reserved.

*A Silence and a Shouting*, Eddie Askew, 1982, The Leprosy Mission International, London, England. All rights reserved.

*A Time to Be Born*, Julie Martin, 1990, Thomas Nelson, Nashville, Tennessee. All rights reserved.

*Whistling in the Dark*, Frederick Buechner, 1988, Harper & Row, New York, New York. All rights reserved.

*Windows of the Soul*, Ken Gire, 1996, Zondervan Publishing, Grand Rapids, Michigan. All rights reserved.

*With Open Hands* by Henri J.M. Nouwen. Copyright 1995 by Ave Maria Press, Notre Dame, IN 46556. Used with permission of publisher.

*The World at One in Prayer*, Daniel Fleming, 1942, Harper & Brothers, New York, New York. All rights reserved.

Gary
Alan
Don
Jimmy